AIRBNB HOSTING GUIDE

How to Make Big Money, Maximize Rental Income, Create Passive Income for Yourself, and Go from Side Hustle to Real Business- Bonus Listing Hacks Included

By: Daniel Stone

© **Copyright 2019 - All rights reserved.**

The content contained within this book may not be reproduced, duplicated or transmitted without direct written permission from the author or the publisher.

Under no circumstances will any blame or legal responsibility be held against the publisher, or author, for any damages, reparation, or monetary loss due to the information contained within this book. Either directly or indirectly.

Legal Notice:

This book is copyright protected. This book is only for personal use. You cannot amend, distribute, sell, use, quote or paraphrase any part, or the content within this book, without the consent of the author or publisher.

Disclaimer Notice:

Please note the information contained within this document is for educational and entertainment purposes only. All effort has been executed to present accurate, up to date, and reliable, complete information. No warranties of any kind are declared or implied. Readers acknowledge that the author is not engaging in the rendering of legal, financial, medical or professional advice. The content within this book has been derived from various sources. Please consult a licensed professional before attempting any techniques outlined in this book.

By reading this document, the reader agrees that under no circumstances is the author responsible for any losses, direct or indirect, which are incurred as a result of the use of information contained within this document, including, but not limited to, — errors, omissions, or inaccuracies.

Table of Contents

Introduction 1

CHAPTER 1: What Is Airbnb? 4

   Why Airbnb Is So Successful? 7
      It Is A Free Market 8
      It Is An Open Platform 8
      Affordable 9
      Socializing 9
      Location 10
   How does Airbnb Work? 11
   Why Host On Airbnb? 12

CHAPTER 2: Airbnb Host Requirements 15

   The Legal Aspects 15
   Privacy Aspect 18
   Invest Time 20
   Get Your Landlord Approval 23
   Authenticity 25

CHAPTER 3: The First Steps 29

   Analyze The Competition 29
   Recognizing Your Target Audience 30
      Property Location 31
      Property Rental 32
   Airbnb Hosting Standards 33
   Update Your Availability 34

Communicate Effectively 36

Stay Committed To Reservations.. 37

Accuracy 39

Protect Your Identity 39

Identify And Avoid Potential Squatters 40

Comforting Your Guests 41

Optimize, Automate, And Even Outsource............................... 42

CHAPTER 4: Is Hosting On Airbnb Safe? 45

CHAPTER 5: Tips For Your Airbnb Listing 48

Your Title 49

Your Description 50

Images 52

Profile 53

CHAPTER 6: Picking Prices 55

Keep The Pricing Low At The Start 56

Don't Stay On The Low Pricing For Too Long 56

Change Your Prices According To The Day Of The Week 57

Seasonal Pricing 57

Smart Pricing 58

CHAPTER 7: Hosting Checklist 59

Setting Of The House 60

Cleaning The House 63

Fixing Hazards 64

Replacing Linens 66

Empty The Refrigerator 67

Secure Your Valuables 68

Make An Extra Guest Key 69

CHAPTER 8: Tips & Tricks For The Host 71

Doing Something Different 71

Make Sure That Your Guest Does Not Wait 72

Pick Up Facility 73

Help Them Get Around 73

Be Different From The Others 74

Ask Your Guest For References 74

CHAPTER 9: Handling A Bad Review On Airbnb . 75

Learn The Truth 75

Believe In Your Apartment 76

The Bad Reviews Help Your Good Reviews 77

Change The Expectations 78

Dealing With Bad Reviews 79
   Don't Panic 79
   Never Remove Bad Reviews 80
   Respond Publicly And Quickly 80
   Learn From Your Reviews 81
   Follow Up 82

Combating Negative Reviews 82
   Mobile Friendly Reviews 83
   Offering Incentives 84
   Ask For Reviews 84

CHAPTER 10: Key Exchange 86
Asking A Friend Or Family Member To Hand Over The Key... 87
Dropping At A Nearby Shop 88
Using An External Service 89
Key Box 90

CHAPTER 11: Becoming A Superhost On Airbnb .. 91
Extra Guest 92
Smoking 94
Eating 95
Cleaning 96
Laundry 97
Gatherings Or Parties 97
Alcohol And Drugs 98
Quiet Hours 99
Children 101
Pets 102

CHAPTER 12: Alternative Methods To Promote Your Listing 104
Create A Story To Support Your Listing 105
Get In Touch With A Lifestyle Blogger Or A Journalist 106
Create A Unique URL 107
Join Vacation Rental Forums 108
Get Listed With Tourism Websites 109

Go Back To Traditional Advertising Techniques 111
Special Offers 112

CHAPTER 13: Airbnb Business Management 113

Use Professional Cleaning Services 113
Outsource As Much As Possible 114
Use Accounting Software 115
Set Aside A Budget Before You Start 115
Prepare Yourself 116
Get A Mentor 116
Set Up A Separate Bank Account 117
Manage Your Property Online 118
Purchase Supplies From One Place 119
Subscriptions 119
Get A Partner 120
Get An Investor 120
Run Your Listing Like A Business 121

CHAPTER 14: Building The Ultimate Host Profile
.... 125

Superhost Evaluations 127

Conclusion 128

Introduction

Airbnb is an amazing marketplace that was founded in 2008. Headquartered in San Francisco, the platform enables people to reserve homes for a holiday by booking an entire apartment, a private room, or even hotel rooms. It is a user-friendly application and is a transparent option that offers freedom to choose from various properties.

There is no denying that Airbnb has become one of the most popular vacation rental platforms. It not only enables people to check out the reviews of other people who stayed in the apartment, but they can also learn more about the surrounding area and the things that they can do. Airbnb was a concept that started off as a small rental solution for people taking holidays and has now become one of the most used platforms to reserve homes.

Airbnb is available in over 191 countries and has over 100 million active users who are constantly looking for places to reserve. The concept of Airbnb is unique, and it's very convenient for people thereby making it a fast growing business. While people have been using Airbnb in order to reserve places to stay on vacation, it's also a great way to earn some money by renting out a spare room or an apartment that you own. People have holiday homes and second homes that they are not using and if you are one of those people and you're looking to earn some extra money then Airbnb is a great platform for you.

The reason Airbnb is gaining so much popularity is because apart from people that are looking to reserve homes for their vacation, there are also a ton of hosts who are registered on the platform and looking to make money. If you're wondering how you can become a part of Airbnb, and make your listing stand out, even with immense competition, then all you need to do is remember that Airbnb is all about convenience and user-friendliness. When you create a listing you need to keep in mind the requirements of the person looking for a place from a vacation perspective so you are able to provide them with what they are looking for.

Finding the perfect balance between creating a profile that is informative and attractive and keeping up to your promises on the platform is something that you need to learn to do, not just virtually but literally as well. Airbnb is transparent not just for the host but also for travelers and that's the reason it's so popular. If you want to list your home and start making substantial earnings from Airbnb you need to make sure that you are on the right path so that you don't make mistakes. Here you will learn how to make the most out of your apartment or the room that you plan on renting out.

Airbnb is designed in a way that it provides people looking for an apartment or room with all the information prior to the reservation. So the more information you provide to the user, the more effective your listing will be. However, creating information that is engaging and interesting is also important. Finding the perfect balance between the information you provide and the attractiveness of the listing is something you need to master.

With this guide, we cover every detail regarding what you need to do to create the perfect Airbnb listing, we will also tell you how to become a host to visitors and guests who will love staying at your apartment or room over and over again. From learning how to start your Airbnb listing, right up to executing it in an effective way and responding to reviews, we have it all covered.

It's time for you to begin your journey and learn how to maximize your earnings with Airbnb.

CHAPTER 1

What Is Airbnb?

So what actually is Airbnb? Airbnb is a platform that helps travelers look for accommodation while taking into account selected criteria. It is also an excellent way for people to make money if they are open to letting a stranger stay in their house. Airbnb is meant to help people look for cheaper and unique accommodations. The hosting experience that travelers look for is something that Airbnb provides. In order to get this experience, travelers pay a small fee and the host also pays a small fee to the platform, in order to get people to stay in their house.

This is a niche market and Airbnb is one of the largest players out there. As we stated before, this platform is active in more than 190 countries and to-date almost 100 million travelers have used Airbnb to find their accommodation. The original concept of Airbnb was to encourage people that had spare rooms in their homes to open the doors to outsiders. The rising prices of hotel rooms and the inflation of prices during the holiday season is what initiated the launch of Airbnb. Travelers have been picking Airbnb as their number one choice for a few years now and this trend doesn't look like it's diminishing. All the more reason for potential hosts to open their doors to travelers from across the world. Apart from providing accommodation, the host can also learn about new cultures and earn extra revenue in the process.

Let's have a look at how Airbnb really started. Back in 2007, Joe Gebbia and Brian Chesky had moved to San Francisco and weren't able to afford the rent for their apartment. They came up with the idea of putting an air mattress in their living room and renting it out to travelers. Initially, the goal was to earn extra money in order to pay the rent. However, they soon saw the potential of this business model and brought in Nathan Blecharczyk as the Chief Technology Officer. This is when the venture began and they named it Airbed & breakfast. They created a small website that offered short term accommodation along with breakfast. Their website Airbedandbreakfast.com was officially launched in August 2008 and they received their very first customers in the summer of 2008. These customers were in town to attend the industrial design conference and they were unable to find affordable lodging in the city and that's the reason they picked Airbedandbreakfast.com.

When they were short of funding the website, they created special edition breakfast cereals and used the then presidential candidate's, John McCain and Barack Obama, as their inspiration. The breakfast cereals were named 'Cap'n

McCains' and 'Obama O's'. The popularity of the cereal boxes soared and over 800 boxes were sold in just two months. These boxes were priced at $40 each and this generated a lot of revenue for the fledgling company. This promotion also caught the attention of Paul Graham, who was a computer programmer, and he invited the founders to attend his training session for startups. This training session was called 'Y Combinator' and it provided the founders with the training they required. The founders were also provided $20,000 in the form of funding in exchange for a small share of the company. The founders used this $20,000 to come to New York and meet potential users and to promote their website. They returned to San Francisco with a very profitable business model and they presented it to West Coast investors.

By March 2009, the website had more than 10,000 users and over 2,500 house listings. This is when the name of the company was shortened and it was converted to airbnb.com. The content of the website also changed and expanded from shared properties to entire apartments and homes along with castles, boats, and private rooms. The company now had 15 people working for them and they were working out of the shared loft apartment in San Francisco that belonged to Chesky and Gebbia. Brian eventually gave up his room in order to make room for the employees and he lived at a lodging that was booked through the Airbnb service. The company received a further $600,000 from Sequoia Capital in April 2009. It also received financial backing in the form of $7.2 million from Greylock Partners in November 2010. The company continued growing and 700,000 nights were been booked on the Airbnb website. By February 2011, Airbnb had its millionth booking and from there on there was no turning back.

Why Airbnb Is So Successful?

A lot of people believe that Airbnb started off as a streamlined app with multiple options to reserve hotel rooms, apartments or a private room that they could rent. The truth is that the Airbnb founders had their share of struggles and it started off as something that was listed on Craigslist before they gained popularity. Today, Airbnb listings are no longer allowed on Craigslist and the business itself has become a $30 billion business with services like no other. The fact that Airbnb manages to cater to the requirements of low budget travelers as well as those looking for luxury accommodations, makes it accessible to all. The filters available on the platform enable people who love traveling to combine affordability with adventure thereby making it extremely trendy.

There are a number of people who wonder why Airbnb is such a popular marketplace and what made it grow so tremendously in such a short time span. Here we have a look at some of the main reasons why Airbnb is in demand and why it is showing no signs of slowing down any time soon.

It Is A Free Market

One of the best things for Airbnb is that it's free to accept for both parties. Unlike most other platforms, users need to register, sign up, and pay a certain fee in order to list their properties on the website. Airbnb allows you to use its platform without charging you any money. If you are a skeptical host and you don't want to invest any money in your business plan then advertising is one of the last things that should be on your mind.

It Is An Open Platform

Airbnb has a streamlined platform which is efficient and you can choose the kind of property that you want to rent out. Whether you have a single bedroom in your house, an entire apartment, or you are a hotel owner who's looking to rent out your hotel room, you can still list your property on Airbnb. If you have free space and you are looking for the best way to utilize the space and begin earning money from it, then you need Airbnb.

The hosts on Airbnb have an easy and convenient way to monetize space that was otherwise empty.

Affordable

Airbnb gives travelers the option of choosing between really reasonable and affordable properties and luxurious multistoried apartments that come with a Jacuzzi. This means people can now rent out their properties irrespective of what kind of property they want to list. If you had a financial crisis recently and you are looking for some way to earn money, you don't have to invest in a new property. All you need to do is clear up your spare bedroom and you can make it Airbnb ready. This is a zero investment business that you can start and it can help you get on your feet.

There are a number of families who register on Airbnb when they have financial problems. In fact, that is how the business idea was conceived. Airbnb listings can help people to cope with their financial problems effectively.

Socializing

One of the reasons people hate staying at a hotel is because it is not warm and welcoming and you do not feel at home. When you have an Airbnb listing, you can provide people with that warm and homely feeling that they usually crave when they are away from home. The reason why Airbnb works so well is because you interact with the guests as much as they want to and it helps them feel welcome in a new country, state, or city. Helping them feel welcome not only lowers anxiety levels but it also gives them the confidence to explore the place a little more. Language isn't something that stops you from communicating with someone because there are amazing translators that are available on your smartphone that can help to communicate with people.

Location

One of the best things about Airbnb is it allows people to search for location-specific apartments or places to rent out. This means that when someone looks for a place in your specific location, your listing will be one of the first listings that will show up. The fact that a person can narrow down their selection to every little detail, including the location and the amenities that are provided, makes it a lot easier for travelers to reserve an Airbnb room rather than look for a cheap hotel or motel.

When it comes to choosing a place to rent on a holiday, flexibility is something that people pay a lot of attention to and Airbnb hosts can be more flexible and understanding than most hotels. This makes it a preferred choice for travelers. It's also more comforting on various levels and this is why people seek that warmth and comfort in the homes they rent out. It is a simple model that works well for both parties.

How does Airbnb Work?

Airbnb works on a model that is not that complicated. There are a number of factors that need to be looked into and the model of Airbnb looks at all of these factors. Here are a few steps in the model that will explain to you how Airbnb actually works:

- It starts off with the host listing the property on Airbnb. This listing will mention all the factors regarding the property such as the amenities that are provided, the location of the property along with the pricing. The host will also need to mention any extra amenities that are provided such as a shared pool or a Jacuzzi on the property. This listing needs to be as accurate as possible to help travelers choose the right property.

- Once the property has been registered, Airbnb hires a freelance photographer. This photographer will go to the property and take high-resolution pictures to upload on the website. This is the responsibility of Airbnb and they pay the freelancer directly for this.

- Once the photographs have been uploaded and the listing has been made available, travelers can then search for the property depending on the city that they want to visit. Travelers will have the option to filter their findings based on the amenities, the location, the pricing as well as many more options.

- Once the traveler selects the property and finalizes details with the host, they will be required to pay the amount that was listed by the host. They will also be asked to pay an additional amount that will be considered a transaction fee.

- Once the payment has been made, the host will have the option of approving or declining the booking. Once this is done, the traveler will stay at the property on the agreed dates and Airbnb will pay the host the agreed amount after deducting a certain commission.

- Once the stay duration has been completed, the host and the traveler will be able to rate each other on the services provided and they will even be able to write their own reviews depending on the kind of experience they had.

Why Host On Airbnb?

There is no denying that Airbnb is a successful concept and it enables hosts to earn money without having to invest a lot of time or resources in order for them to begin earning enough to support their family and secure their future. There are a lot of positive attributes that Airbnb has but there are also a few things that the host should take care of. While it may seem exciting to you to take the plan and become an Airbnb host, it is important to take your time before making your decision. You need to take into consideration the various pros and cons when deciding whether to become an Airbnb host.

It may sound all hunky dory at the start and registering may look like a cakewalk but you need to understand that when you open your doors to somebody new, there are a number of risks that you should know about. Airbnb takes into consideration the risk factors and this is why they have a strong legal team which will help you. Airbnb makes sure that they adhere to the various rules of the country that you are in. Depending on where you stay, you will have to make sure that you check the rules of that country. There will also be a number of scenarios that you may come across and these include your house being trash or even products or goods and valuables being stolen, but let's not forget that these scenarios amount to less than 1% of the overall experience on Airbnb.

Overall, it's a safe platform to use and Airbnb tries its best to keep the travelers as well as the host as safe and comfortable as possible so that they have a pleasant experience using the marketplace. Before you decide that you want to become a host, it is important to keep yourself informed about the various risks involved so you can protect yourself and make an informed choice. For instance, if you are a single woman and you would like to rent out a spare room in your apartment it would always make more sense for you to rent your apartment to women only, just to stay safe.

Once you have decided that you want to become an Airbnb

host, and you have taken your first step towards what could be a highly profitable business, you need to select the pricing for your listing. An Airbnb host is allowed to choose the price they would like to put on their apartment or room that they are renting and they can even change the prices depending on the season or the time of the week (weekend listing prices are usually higher).

One of the best things about being a host on Airbnb is you can learn to socialize with people from all over the world and get to interact with people from various nationalities and learn about their cultural background. When you have established connections all over the world, it helps you to grow and learn more about different parts of the world. Airbnb is not just for frequent travelers but also for business people and when you get a chance to interact with people belonging to different walks of life, it helps you understand and blend in with society.

Many people look at Airbnb as a source of passive income but let's not forget that it isn't just a way for you to earn extra money, it's also a way for you to change the way you live and look at society. Instead of looking at an empty space you own, you can fill it with warmth and comfort and make it a great source of income that can help you earn money regularly without too much effort.

CHAPTER 2

Airbnb Host Requirements

Now that you want to sign up with Airbnb, all you need to do is follow the steps in order for you to become a successful host. There are various things that you need to keep in mind and ensure that you have in place so that you become a good host. Once you download the Airbnb app, all you need to do is sign up by using your email address or even your Facebook or Google account. It is a simple process and once you sign up, you can then begin your journey of becoming a successful Airbnb host. There are many things that you need to keep in mind in order for you to ensure that you are on the right track. Here let's take a look at every little detail you need to follow in order for you to start your hosting experience on the right foot.

The Legal Aspects

Airbnb is available in multiple countries and the rules for each country are different. This is completely dependent upon the house sharing laws in your state or city and the rules that you need to follow. When you download your Airbnb app, you can go on to the rules and regulations section and make sure that you read the details correctly and in-depth. There is a lot of information and you need to make sure that you have everything in place so that you do not break any laws. Airbnb has some restrictions in the United States which do not allow you to share your home with a certain number of people and in some areas you need to even apply for a license before you begin your Airbnb journey.

If you want to start hosting on Airbnb you need to make sure that you do it in a step by step process so that there are no complications. While Airbnb is free and doesn't have too many restrictions in most countries, there are still a few rules and regulations that you need to follow if you want to make sure that you do not do anything that could get you in trouble with the law.

As we mentioned, some cities or states even require the host to get a license or a permit before they begin hosting on the platform. In case you live in any of those areas you need to get your license sorted out. A lot of people believe that they can host on Airbnb on the quiet, without having to follow the rules and regulations even if they are simple. If you plan on staying an Airbnb host for a long time, it is highly recommended that you stay in accordance with every law, even if it is something as small as the number of days that you can rent out property to a traveler or the number of people that are allowed to stay in your apartment. You never really know what could go against you and if you end up on the wrong side of the law, you may have to permanently take down your listing from Airbnb and you will no longer be able to make any money out of it.

People who sign up on Airbnb and do not follow these rules and regulations usually end up paying hefty penalties and fines and they are taken off the platform permanently. It is quite a daunting experience and not something that anyone would want to go through. While it may seem exciting and you may want to begin your journey as an Airbnb host as soon as possible, it is highly recommended that you take your time and learn the laws before you actually list your property. It also makes it more convenient for you to confidently list your property without the risk of anyone pointing a finger at you or saying that you are doing something that is wrong or illegal. While Airbnb is available in most countries there are also countries that have strict rules with regards to short term leasing and if you belong to one of those countries then you may want to reconsider becoming an Airbnb host.

There are also various occupancy taxes and other such details that you should take full responsibility for prior to listing your property on Airbnb. You also need to make sure that all the bills are cleared for the property before you list it for rental. The last thing you want is for your utility connection to be cut off when you have a traveler living inside your apartment.

Privacy Aspect

As an Airbnb host, you will need to take into consideration the privacy of the traveler who rents out your property, even if it is a shared room. Airbnb is very particular about the privacy provided to people, even if it is in a shared apartment or simply a bed that is rented out for the night. The reason this is so essential is because it helps to lower the risk of anything that could go wrong between both parties and also keeps the host as well as the guests safe. As an Airbnb host, it is definitely recommended that you get surveillance cameras for all common areas such as the common room, the corridor, and the entrance of the apartment. However, you need to make sure that you know your limits and you do not install cameras where it is not required and this means the bedrooms or the toilets and bathrooms. If for some reason you install cameras or surveillance in places that may invade the privacy of a guest then you could be breaking the law and you could get into trouble. If you have surveillance and it is in particular areas around the apartment, it is important for you to make sure that you mention this while discussing your property on Airbnb. The reason it is important for you to list the surveillance devices and their location is to respect the privacy of the guest.

When you create a listing on Airbnb the one thing that you need to remember is to be as honest and clear with your guests as possible and this includes letting them know what is and isn't included in the property. If you provide your guests with incomplete or incorrect information about the property, they have the right to cancel the reservation and request a refund. In such situations, you will have to pay penalties to Airbnb and if this occurs multiple times, you may end up losing your listing on Airbnb permanently. As a host, you must understand that your guest is looking for a place they feel comfortable staying, which is why they didn't choose a hotel and the one thing that you have to make sure you provide them is privacy and comfort. It's also important to know where your boundaries are drawn and take the safety of the guest into consideration.

The reason it is important to understand the value of security, as well as privacy, is because sometimes your guests can arrive at odd hours because of time differences between two countries or other reasons. While it makes you feel safe to have surveillance installed because you know who is coming in and out, it's critical that the guest arriving is fully aware of the camera placement so that they do not feel uncomfortable during their stay. A lot of time travelers like to get certain information about a property just because they know what they are comfortable or uncomfortable with and hosts tend to hide details like a surveillance camera because they believe that it may scare the guests away. You need to understand that the guest also respects your security and need for surveillance, as long as it is in places that do not interfere with their stay or discomforts them in any way. In fact, most guests tend to choose places that have surveillance devices because they feel more secure, especially when they are lone travelers.

Invest Time

If you are serious about becoming an Airbnb host and make a profit from it then you need to make sure that you give it enough time to grow and become successful. When you first download the Airbnb app you are going to see multiple listings and it may excite you just knowing how many times a property has been booked in the past. Just because these listings were successful doesn't necessarily mean that you will start getting people to rent your property the very same day you list it. Some places require some time to gain popularity but once the tourist season begins in your country or city, the chances of your property getting a traveler automatically increases.

You also need to make sure that your property gets the kind of exposure that it needs on Airbnb. When there are multiple listings that are similar to yours, it is important that you put in a little time to understand what you have gotten yourself into, the kind of competition that you face, as well as the pricing of the property. If you do not invest time and research effectively you may end up listing your property at a very low price or at a very high price, both of which will result in a loss for you.

Once your listing is live, give your Airbnb listing at least an hour a day. The app is very convenient to use and this means that the minute someone shows interest in your listing you will get a notification on your mobile phone and you can choose to reply to the inquiry almost instantly. When somebody shows an interest in a property, they tend to check out multiple listings at the same time so that they can find someone who responds to them quickly. The host that replies the quickest is considered efficient. The thing with an Airbnb listing is that people don't really check so much for the location as much as they check for a host being warm and responsive.

A great way for you to make sure that you are providing your guest with the right information as soon as possible is to have a template ready with certain question and answers so that you simply copy and paste the answers whenever a guest has requested a certain kind of information. You should also provide almost all of the information on your listing itself so that there are not too many questions that need to be answered. Even if you do provide all the information to your guest there will be different queries that people come up with from time to time. For instance, if you have a property listed for four guests and there are five people who are looking for a room, they will message you on Airbnb and ask whether you are ready to change the listing a little bit for them. This is something you can take a call on, depending on where you live and whether or not you are allowed to have more than four people at your place. If it's allowed and if you are able to provide them with the comfort they seek, then you can go ahead but if you cannot then you should learn how to politely decline.

One of the smartest ways to get more people to stay comfortably in your apartment would be to get extra mattresses and a sofa bed in the living area. However, all of this information needs to be provided carefully and you also have to be available to chat with your guests from time to time to ensure that they have an amazing stay. All the information provided to your potential guest must be clear and this includes how you will handle the cleaning and all the little details including the time that they can check-in and check-out. One of the most common request guests have is an early check-in and a late checkout. Some Airbnb hosts are accommodating while others tend to ask the guests to pay a little extra so that they can provide them with this service. Whether you want to charge them extra for half a day or whether you want to provide them with the room for free, it is a choice that you are left to make but you also need to remember that Airbnb travelers tend to recommend places on the platform. If you want to get strong and positive feedback from the guests that stay at your place, you may want to provide them with specialized service. When you are just starting on Airbnb and you treat your guests' right, it will start reflecting on your listing and this will help your listing become a successful one.

Get Your Landlord Approval

It may surprise you but there are a number of hosts for Airbnb who don't really own a house or an apartment but still manage to list on Airbnb. If you are wondering how they managed to do this then consider this: if you have a large apartment that you have rented out and you were sharing it with a friend but they have moved out and you need someone to cover their share of the rent, then a smart way for you to do this would be to list the apartment on Airbnb. It's a great way to make a lot more than you could actually imagine and you will also manage to balance out your routine expenses by doing this.

However, since this is not your property it is important for you to inform your landlord about your choices and make sure that you get their permission before you set up your Airbnb account. It is very tempting for you to go behind their back and do this on the quiet but Airbnb is a very popular platform and it will not take long for your landlord to see their own apartment being listed there. Also, it's quite difficult to be sneaky when you constantly have guests checking into your and leaving your apartment. In order for you to avoid any complications, make sure that your contract contains all the details of your subleasing and how you will be leasing it out on the platform. While you do not need to get into the financials with your landlord you definitely need to keep them informed with regards to what you are doing and get their permission so that you are able to do it regularly. Most landlords don't really have a problem with you renting or subleasing an apartment or a room, as long as they receive their rent on a regular basis. It is just better that you get this done at the start of your listing so that you avoid complications with your landlord later on. The last thing you want is for your landlord to ask you to move out of your apartment for breaking the rules.

Authenticity

Listing on Airbnb is exciting and you may want to list your property at a really high price so that you can get the maximum revenue out of your listing. One of the most important things to focus on while listing on Airbnb is the authenticity of your property. Sometimes the property rates fluctuate so much that an apartment a few blocks away from yours may be priced at almost double what you have priced your property at. If you want to be a reliable Airbnb host, then the most important thing for you to consider is providing your travelers with a 'value for money' service so that they are happy with their stay and they leave a good review for the property. If you list your property at an extremely high price, it will make it difficult for them to think it was a good deal and this could reflect badly on their review for your property. If you want people to enjoy living in your home and you want to make sure that they are leaving with a good feeling, then accuracy and authenticity are really important.

While providing them with details such as your property being next to or near something, it's important to give them the exact location so they know what they are getting into and whether or not it will be a feasible location for them to choose. You have to remember that most travelers come from a different city and sometimes a different country so they are looking for places that make it easy for them to travel and when you provide them the right information then they can plan their stay accordingly. Do not let small things get in the way of providing people with the right details.

If you plan on being an Airbnb host long term, it means you need to be honest with your travelers and give them the information that they are seeking. Sometimes guests even tend to ask you the distance from your apartment to certain places and a lot of Airbnb hosts try to cover up these facts simply because they want to get the person to come and stay with them. This is something that you shouldn't do. When you are honest with your guests, they will adjust their travel plans to stay in your apartment. Also, if they ever need to come back to the city and your property is listed, they will definitely come back and stay in your apartment.

Another thing that you should be very careful of when listing your property on Airbnb is to make sure that you provide correct descriptions and actual pictures of the place you are renting out. Airbnb provides the host with this by sending in a photographer to take pictures without charging them. This will help you to provide your travelers with the right information.

You should get good quality pictures of your property and make sure that you use the right images. If you are not too sure how your property will look in pictures then you can add a few minor touches to the property to make it look more appealing. We are in a day and age where there's so much information available on the Internet that with a little time invested on photography tips and tricks, you can spruce up even the most basic space and turn it into something unique, comforting, and warm. Before you list your property on Airbnb, you need to look at the property and ask yourself whether you are happy renting out the property at the price you are considering. If you think that you will be happy then great but if you think it's not worth it then it's always recommended to do something to spruce it up. A few details here and there could add a warm touch to the entire space and create a welcome environment for the guests.

Remember, pictures are one of the first things that people look at before they rent a property. This means you need to put in a lot of time and effort when it comes to getting clean, accurate, and beautiful pictures that can capture the true sense of your property and make it stand out. Bright lighting, linens, and fabrics that stand out and colors that pop are a few things that people definitely get attracted to and these are minor details that can help you get more travelers to visit your place in comparison to others. While you don't have to create a luxurious living environment you can definitely create something that makes a person want to rent your property just because it looks different from the rest and is beautiful.

Cleanliness is also very important when it comes to renting out properties and in order for you to be a long-term host on Airbnb, you need to make sure that you provide them with continuous electricity, heating and cooling solutions, running water, and the bare necessities.

When you manage to get all of these aspects right, not only do you manage to rent out your property more regularly but you will feel confident in doing so because you know you're providing them with value for money. They are benefiting by renting your property and you are benefiting by getting people to stay regularly. This also reduces the risk of a bad review because you know you have provided exactly what you have listed and people will enjoy the experience when they spend time at your place.

Don't let temptation get the better of you. Provide a living space that people can actually comment on. When you look at your apartment, ask yourself if you would be happy to rent it out at a price that you are asking for and if it puts a smile on your face then it's a great start to your new venture but if not, then try making a few adjustments and changes before you list it.

CHAPTER 3

The First Steps

If you have decided that you want to list your property on Airbnb then here are a few things that you need to take care of. You need to consider what the market is doing and how to make your listing stand out from the competition. Here are a few things that you need to keep in mind that will help you get your listing right on Airbnb.

Analyze The Competition

Researching your competition and analyzing what they are doing is extremely important. It's not that difficult to research your competition on Airbnb. All you need to do is search for similar listings in your local area and you will be able to come up with your competitor's listings. You need to filter the listings based on the amenities that you are providing such as bathrooms, bedrooms, kitchen facilities, and other additional amenities such as a garden or a pool. You need to look at how your competition is listing their property and you may find some inspiration for your listing as well. This will help you stay ahead of the competition and it will help you get better results than them. When you are researching your competition, you need to also check on their prices. If their prices are too low, you need to check the facilities they are providing. It does not necessarily mean that you need to adjust your pricing as low as your competition. It is important to price your apartment just right so that your guests do not feel that they are overpaying.

Recognizing Your Target Audience

Whenever you start listing your property on Airbnb you always need to keep your target audience in mind. Identify who your ideal guest would be and then target your marketing strategies to your audience. If you feel that your property is suitable for youngsters then you will have to direct your marketing strategies to reach such an audience. For example, you can show students having fun in your house or jumping in the pool when they are living in your apartment. If you feel that your apartment is suitable for a family then you need to show pictures that are more family oriented rather than showing students jumping in your pool. Similarly, if you feel like your apartment is suitable for retired people then you will need to put appropriate pictures of the house. If you are not sure who your target audience may be, then you will need to keep two factors in mind: your property's location and your property's rental.

Property Location

Your property location will usually decide the kind of visitors that you receive. You need to take note of the kind of people that live in your neighborhood as these are the kind of visitors that will be interested in your apartment. Most travelers select a specific area because of the facilities nearby and the kind of people that stay there. People usually have just two purposes for visiting a country: it could be for business purposes or for a vacation. You also need to check if there is a famous landmark near your house, a tourist attraction, or maybe an event like a concert that is taking place near your apartment. Ask yourself the following questions in order to figure out your rental location and understand your target audience:

- What are the kind of people that live in your neighborhood?
- Is your area full of business people or are there students living in your area or are there families living there?
- What are the tourist attractions that are near your area?
- Are there any nightlife spots or sports stadiums that attract people regularly to your area?
- How many hotels are located near your apartment?

The answer to the last question is extremely important. This is because if there are few hotels located near the apartment then you have the potential to earn a lot of money through your Airbnb listing. A lot of travelers look at the best options when they are traveling to a specific area and if there are too many hotels then your Airbnb pricing may not be able to compete with their pricing. However when there are very few hotels or no hotels in your area then you will be able to get sufficient people to rent out your apartment.

Property Rental

Now that you know the kind of people that live in your area and the kind of travelers that may come to stay in your property, you can figure out who your potential guests may be by thinking what your property has to offer and what price that you want to offer it at. These are the questions you will need to ask yourself in order to figure out your property type:

- Are you offering an entire apartment or are you offering a shared room?
- Will your guests have access to the laundry facilities?
- Will your guests be able to use your kitchen facilities?
- If you have a pool, will you allow your guests to use it?
- Are there parking facilities for your guests?
- Do you allow pets in your house?

- Is your apartment located in a well-lit area?

Once you have the answers to all of these questions, you will be able to think about your target market and decide the pricing for your property. As we stated above, research is extremely important and you need to know what your competition is doing before you decide your pricing.

Airbnb Hosting Standards

When you become a host on Airbnb one of the most important things that you need to pay attention to is the hosting standard. There are various requirements that guests look for when reserving a home on Airbnb and the more likely you are to provide them with exactly what they are looking for, the higher the chances that you will be in business for a long time.

If you plan on renting out your property just a couple of times so that you can make a quick buck then the standards will not play an important role in your life. However, if you want to stay an Airbnb host for the long term and earn a good amount of money so you can secure your future, it is very important that you take into consideration the several hosting standards that Airbnb needs their hosts to follow.

One of the main mottos of Airbnb reads 'hospitality is the secret to success' and this simply means that they want every host to provide the best possible experience to a traveler and make them feel welcome in a new place. When you begin your journey as an Airbnb host, the one thing you should try to focus on is to provide your guests with quality services, even if it means cutting down on your profit a little. If you want more from your rental business, you also need to give back to it every now and then. No good deed goes unnoticed and when you work hard towards keeping a beautiful environment and meet the hosting standard, not only do you get better ratings but your property becomes highly noticeable.

Think about what you look for when you plan on renting a property on Airbnb. Does the rating play a huge role in determining whether or not you will go ahead with the booking? While hosts tend to ignore the importance of reviews on the Airbnb platform this is probably one of the most essential factors that every host should consider and if you want a high rating, then quality standards and hosting standards play a huge role. The better the hospitality, the better the reviews and this means more guests which eventually transcends into higher income. When you begin your journey with Airbnb not only do you need to focus on the hosting standard but you need to make sure that you maintain consistency with your service so that your ratings do not fluctuate.

Update Your Availability

We have discussed this before and I'm saying it again, just so that you remember the importance of dedicating at least an hour a day towards your Airbnb listing. The reason you need to do this is because it gives you enough time to update and mark your calendar for the days that are blocked. This is important mainly because it helps to exclude people who are looking to rent your property on the days that you already have bookings and it saves you the effort of having to communicate with these people in the first place. Secondly, it provides you wider exposure to people who are looking to book a place well in advance and when people notice that you have multiple bookings and your calendar is blocked, it is easy for them to assume that your listing is popular.

When you mark your calendar, you should always try to keep at least a one day gap between two bookings. The reason you should do this is because it gives you enough time to visit the property personally and check whether or not everything is in place. While it is not common for guests to create a problem in a rented apartment there may be times when your guests have been irresponsible and messed up your place. Handling a booking immediately after the last guest has checked out increases the risk of the property not being up to standard for the next guest. This does not go down well with guests because you need to remember that the first impression is the last impression. That one day that you give yourself in between allows you the time to prepare and make it look beautiful again so that when somebody enters, they feel welcome and warm.

Communicate Effectively

There is no denying that the best way to crack a deal is to communicate. This doesn't just hold true for the host and guest prior to the reservation but right up until the time they leave your home. The more you communicate with your guests, the more it helps to solve most of the problems that they may face while they are staying at your place. Although you may try your level best to provide them with everything that they need, there are times when guests feel a little frustrated, maybe because they are in a new location or because they can't understand what people around them are saying. When you offer help to guests, it helps them to calm down.

When you communicate with your guests you should always have a list of questions ready to ask them and provide information that you want them to know before they come to stay at your property. One of the most important things that you should always check with your guests is the check-in and checkout time. It is important that you have a certain time set for the check-in and checkout but if your guests request an early check-in or a late checkout you need to communicate with them and let them know whether or not this is going to be possible and if you will be charging for that service. In case you are planning on early check-ins or late checkouts and you have a caretaker who handles the property for you, you also need to make sure that you provide them with all the information with regards to the booking and the time of arrival and departure.

In cases where you communicate in a different language to your guest you shouldn't stress. This is because Airbnb offers a translation service on the app itself which enables two people to communicate effectively even if they do not speak the same language. Using the chat app to send messages back and forth makes it easy and convenient for both people to be understood. It is also safer because everything that you say to the guest and the guest says back to you is on record with Airbnb.

Stay Committed To Reservations

There are times when your place will be booked well in advance and you will get inquiries from people who are willing to offer more for your apartment, if you are ready to rent it out to them at the last minute. This may seem really tempting and you may want to go ahead and cancel the prior booking just so that you can get more money from the new guests; this is something you should avoid doing. Not only does it reflect badly on you as a host but you will become unreliable, which Airbnb notices. When you start canceling reservations without a reason, your profile automatically gets flagged over and over again and you may end up losing your rights to become a host on Airbnb permanently. If you are not comfortable with reserving your property three or four months in advance then you can always keep it open for a month or two but when you are an Airbnb host and you are looking for a long-term business you shouldn't be looking to make a little extra money; instead you should look to make regular money. In case something goes wrong and you have to cancel your reservation with a guest, the best thing to do is cancel it well in advance so that the guests gets their money back. If a guest needs to cancel their booking then there is not much you can do about it. All you need to do is open your listing and make it available at a higher price for the people who are looking for properties at the last moment and are willing to spend more money on a reservation.

Accuracy

Airbnb is an open platform. When you see that people listed in neighboring areas are getting paid higher for a property that they have listed, you may want to try and cover up the flaws in your rental property just so you can get that high price. This is something that you should avoid, not only because it's wrong and unethical, but also because the guest will eventually learn the truth about your property and this will come up on your profile. When Airbnb notices that you have not been honest with the details provided, your account will be suspended and you will lose the chance of earning with Airbnb.

Protect Your Identity

As a host on Airbnb one of the most important things to keep in mind is that there are going to be a number of people who would want to steal your identity and take advantage of the opportunity in front of them. While you do need to provide specific details to people who are looking to rent properties on Airbnb, it is highly recommended that you do not give out too much of your information and this includes your personal contact information. Airbnb is a transparent platform that allows people to get in touch with guests on the platform itself and this is a two-way communication which is effective and easy. There is an app that can be downloaded on your

Smartphone and people are able to use the application no matter where they are. As much as possible it is highly recommended that you do not provide any of your personal details unless the reservation is confirmed. Once the guest books your place, you may want to provide them with a contact number so that they can get in touch with you while they are traveling and when they arrive.

You may also want to have a separate phone number just for Airbnb so that you can differentiate between your personal and professional life and people that come and stay in your apartment cannot get your personal details or your private phone number. While it is important for you to take care of the privacy of your guests you also need to remember that you shouldn't share any of your information that could open the door to potential issues.

Identify And Avoid Potential Squatters

Airbnb is an amazing place for travelers and one of the best things about being a host on Airbnb is that you have the opportunity to rent people your apartment for a short time span. The minute somebody tries to book your Airbnb listing for more than 30 days, this could eat into your profits, not only monetary but also because you have less opportunity to gain exposure. While there are limited chances of getting a squatter on Airbnb, it is still possible and while it may seem like a great way to get money, it doesn't always work out in your favor. If there is one person who stays in your apartment for a long time, it will not provide you with any exposure on the platform and your room will be reserved for all the days that they stay. The longer they stay in your home, the higher the chances of something going wrong. This means that it will affect your profile in a negative way. Shorter stays are better and they help your profile to grow. This is why you may want to avoid long term reservations.

Comforting Your Guests

When your guests come from places that are across the globe, there are going to be differences in the time zones and this means that they need to feel comfortable and warm when they reach your apartment. Remember that the new time zone may take a toll on them and they are most likely going to be jet lagged and frustrated because of the long travel. In such a situation the smartest thing for you to do would be to offer them a warm place so that it makes them feel relaxed. You don't have to go out of your way by spending too much money or putting in too much effort in order for them to feel this way. All you need to do is provide them with special care that can make their life a little easier. For example, if they are arriving early in the morning then you can arrange a nice breakfast for them so that they can explore the city on a full stomach. If you interact with your guests you will know what they are looking for and when they visit you already know the purpose of their visit. If they are looking to check out new places then giving them some information about the city and how to get around conveniently is something that will definitely help them.

If you get a single female traveler, you may want to try and provide her with safe solutions to get around the city so that they are confident during their visit and nothing goes wrong. While it is not your responsibility to ensure the safety of your guests once they leave your property, they will feel more confident if you help them. They will also share the feedback on the platform.

A long journey can be stressful and creates a lot of chaos and anxiety amongst guests. You may want to do some things to help them ease their stress levels and feel relaxed as soon as they reach the property. Arranging for soothing packets of tea or coffee always works well because these can refresh your guests. You may also want to keep a music system or a radio in the apartment so they can connect their phones and listen to the music of their choice. While it is impossible for you to keep a huge collection of different kinds of music for people belonging to different countries, you can definitely keep a device that can connect to a mobile phone that plays the songs of their choice.

Optimize, Automate, And Even Outsource

The idea of being able to rent property on Airbnb is useful when you have little free time and you want to do different things in life. While Airbnb is considered to be a nice source of income, you need to make the most of the listing because everything else is handled by the platform itself. When you have a successful listing, putting in an hour a day is all you need in order for you to run a successful business on Airbnb and become a popular host.

While it is great to have your own Airbnb listing for one particular property, it could get a little daunting when you have multiple properties to handle. In such situations, not only do you need to learn how to optimize your properties more effectively but you also need to learn how to automate processes and outsource certain services when required.

Airbnb has amazing automated services so there is not a lot of effort that you need to put into listings manually. However, the one thing that you should always remember is to check your calendar and block the dates that the property has already been booked for.

Outsourcing is another important element that you should consider when you become an Airbnb host. While it is not compulsory for you to outsource all your jobs to somebody else, it is definitely recommended when you handle more than one property. The reason it is important for you to outsource some of the services such as house cleaning and caretaking is because this takes away a lot of the responsibility and allows you to manage your finances effectively so you can consider investing in new properties to rent out on Airbnb. When you hire a caretaker to look after your property, not only does this help to ensure that standards are met, but it also helps to keep your property a lot cleaner. You review the cleanliness and availability of amenities in your house on a regular basis and the housekeeper is somebody who will ensure all of this is regularly updated and taken care of. A housekeeper also comes in really handy when you need somebody to look into minor repair work in the house such as changing light bulbs or calling in a plumber or an electrician to get a job done. It helps you to systematically arrange the various things that need to be done and it increases your credibility as a host.

CHAPTER 4

Is Hosting On Airbnb Safe?

When you become a host on Airbnb it's very common for you to wonder whether or not it is a safe place for you to do business or if there are various risks involved with it. Since the concept is not that old, there are a number of people who think that Airbnb is not safe and there are a number of complications that you could come across when renting property on the platform. However, Airbnb is just as safe as any reservation that somebody would make at a hotel. There is, of course, the chance of you coming across an extremely rude guest or tourist who tries to behave in an appropriate manner with you but that is also the case with a hotel. If you are worried about your place getting completely trashed and something going drastically wrong when you become a host on Airbnb then this is the last thing that you need to worry about because there is a very slim chance of you coming across someone who will behave in this manner when they rent on Airbnb. Yes, there are going to be people who are a little messy and enjoy having parties when they are renting the place but again that doesn't really happen often, and Airbnb is safer when compared to other options that you come across.

Airbnb hosts also stress about what would happen if the tourists do not leave the premises once they have completed their stay and what needs to be done in order for them to be moved out of the place. When you choose people to stay in your apartment you can always read their reviews and if you are not comfortable with what you've read you can choose to politely decline their reservation. Airbnb does not accept bad customers and this helps people to maintain a lot of transparency. This keeps the platform clean and in cases where someone gets a bad review then they are suspended from the platform. The guest, as well as the host, is required to give reviews. This is a two-way street thereby making it just as safe for the host as it is for the guest. Since all the communication happens on Airbnb it is a safe and secure mode of communication and Airbnb keeps an eye on every little detail. Even the payments that take place on Airbnb happen through the platform so this is something the host does not need to worry about.

While you can definitely share your contact details once the booking is confirmed the entire communication takes place on the Airbnb platform itself. Airbnb is always in the loop with regards to what's happening. The platform is highly secure and this makes it very easy for hosts to receive money and make a booking. Once the guest transfers the amount on Airbnb, the host receives the complete payment one day prior to the guest arriving at their home. This means that you don't have to worry about not getting paid.

If you are worried about the guest not leaving the premises once their stay is over, this is something that you do not have to worry about because you hand the guest a spare set of keys to the apartment. If they exceed the duration of their reservation you can always change the lock. When you have a conversation with the guests and you feel that they are not reliable you can definitely choose to cancel their reservation immediately. You have no obligation to accept every reservation that comes your way and in cases where a guest makes you feel uneasy, you can definitely cancel their booking.

If for some reason, you feel Airbnb is not taking responsibility for your property and there could be damages that could cost you a lot of money, Airbnb provides hosts with a guarantee and insurance of $100,000. This is called the 'Peace of mind' guarantee. This guarantee covers hosts all over the world in case the guest has incurred damages. There are certain items Airbnb does not cover. Therefore, as a host, you may want to have your own private insurance for your property as well.

CHAPTER 5

Tips For Your Airbnb Listing

Becoming a host on Airbnb may seem exciting and there will be a number of plans that you have already made for yourself believing that you will be a successful host. However, you need to remember there are a ton of Airbnb hosts who have the exact same dream and believe they are going to gain a lot of popularity on the platform too. If you want to become a successful Airbnb host it is important that you take your time to understand exactly what the platform requires you to do and what the guests expect from you. While there are no hard and fast rules with regards to what does and does not work, you may want to think of yourself as a customer who is looking to rent a property on a short term basis and take into consideration the various requirements when you plan on going on a business trip or a vacation with your family. Once you sign up on Airbnb, you are taken to the registration page where you need to make sure you get all your details filled in correctly. People can check your property and decide whether or not it's the kind of property they would like to rent. This may all be very overwhelming and you may not know how to make your listing effective. This walkthrough will help you list your apartment on Airbnb in the most effective way.

Your Title

The title of your listing needs to provide the guest with all the possible information that they are looking for. When somebody reads the title, they need to be able to make a decision with regards to whether or not this is what they want, almost instantly. A smart way to create a title would be to provide your customers with about 80% of the information in a short and engaging line. For example: A 3 BHK apartment with a pool opposite Central Park.

Not only does this listing clearly describe the apartments but it also lets the guests know certain details such as the pool and the location, thereby making it an easy decision for the guest to make. When a guest is looking for a property to rent, they often already have a location in mind. Providing them with a hint of the location in your title always works in your favor because it helps them to narrow down their selection. You also need to make sure that your title is not very long so it can be read effectively. When the title is too long, people tend to lose interest. The title should fit into a mobile screen without having to scroll up and down to read what is written. It should be a complete title and guests should be able to read it even while they are scrolling through multiple listings whithout making them click on the listing to see the complete title. The title needs to grab their attention so you need to be creative, quirky, and innovative with your title ideas. Your title is the main brand for your space so make sure that you add all the USP's to your title that will help you sell more.

Your Description

The description of your listing is a detailed description of the property, where you need to include every minor detail and the amenities that you provide. This is necessary because most guests are very picky about the kind of services that are available in the property and they want to know everything, including the balcony space. It is also important for you to list the number of bathrooms in the apartment along with the ones that are attached to a bedroom and the ones that are commonly shared with the living area.

If you are not providing a complete property then you may want to consider providing a refrigerator and an induction stove top in the kitchen so that guests can prepare their own meals. All this information should also be included in the description because it adds to the attractiveness of the listing.

If you are providing your guests with an induction stove you also need to provide them with utensils to cook. Even if you choose not to provide them with an induction in the kitchen you still need to provide them with cutlery and crockery so that they can bring food from outside and eat at home. People who don't carry much, such as budget travelers, look for these amenities so providing them with kitchen space and cooking area is a definite unique selling point that you should take into consideration. If you do not want to go to the hassle of providing a gas stove then induction is always the safest bet.

A television is another thing that you should try and include in the listing because people tend to spend a lot of time in front of the TV and even if they are only at home for a few hours they would still like to enjoy watching TV.

The one thing to remember is that you enter every little detail about the property including a workspace that you may have set up. When you enter the description, make sure that whatever details you enter in the description are actual facts about your property and there's nothing exaggerated or made up. Your description is like a company profile and every guest is going to read through it carefully before they make a final decision. So make it as innovative and interesting as possible.

Images

Photographs are really important for your Airbnb listing. You'll want to get the best possible photographs for the listing. Before getting photos taken, ensure that the apartment is clean and there is a lot of natural light flowing through it so that it is shown in its true color and element. When you plan on getting the photography done for your apartment you may want to pick bright colors rather than pale shades of white and grey because these don't really stand out in the images and they won't reflect the true essence of the property. When taking these photographs try to get a clear picture of all the amenities that you provide and this includes the bed and the refrigerator that is available. The photographer's services are free so you don't have to worry about paying any money to get pictures taken.

Every Airbnb host has the right to set their own house rules and this means that they can choose the rules that the guests need to follow. This includes deciding whether or not you would like to allow people to have alcohol inside the apartment or whether you are comfortable with a group of teenagers coming and partying in your apartment. Some people have a shared space that they would like to rent out but they still have a separate entrance to enter and this enables the guest to come in and out whenever they want. However, if there is no separate entrance for the shared apartment then you may want to mention the time that you want the guest to be home so that they do not disrupt your routine. While you may believe that this is being a little harsh on your guest and you do not want to impose your rules on them, it's really important especially when it's a shared apartment. Unless there are certain rules that you lay out, the guests may believe that no matter what they do, you are fine with it and that's when they begin to get on your nerves. Your house rules should also state the number of people that you would allow to stay in the apartment. The rule of thumb is to accommodate two people per bedroom and if you have a common sleeping space in the hall or the living area then you could count two more people for that area as well. Whether or not you allow guests to come and visit is something that you should make a call on. During the day you should also make it clear that the guests need to take the garbage out.

Profile

It is important for you to protect your privacy but it's also important for you to give your guests details about who you are and a little about your background. If you are a local then you may want to stress the fact that you have lived your entire life in that particular area and you will be able to provide them with information with regards to traveling, getting around the city, and even places to visit. Try to make your profile female friendly and let people know that you are always available to help. It's essential for you to maintain transparency with visitors and let them know what to expect from you. You also need to let them know if you will be handling the listing on your own or if you have a caretaker that will be in charge. In case you have a caretaker to handle the home, then it's necessary for you to make sure the contact details of the caretaker are provided to the guests and provide the caretaker with the guest's number so that they can get in touch with each other. If you are not going to be available then you need to let the guest know about this in advance because they will expect to see you unless you tell them otherwise.

CHAPTER 6

Picking Prices

Now we will look at the pricing of your apartment in detail. You should not just look at the pricing from a profit perspective. You should list your apartment at just the right price so that people will come to your property again and again. For this, you will need to understand the market and understand the potential that your apartment has. If you overprice your apartment, there is a very good chance that your vacancy rate will be very high. Even if somebody does book your apartment, there could be a possibility that they will be very unhappy and they may complain about being overcharged. If you mark your pricing too low then there is a chance that you will be losing money and you could even attract guests that will cause damage to your house. Finding the right balance between overpricing and underpricing is something that you need to figure out through a lot of analysis. If you are a first-time host then you may have underestimated the operating costs or you may be expecting very high profits from the very first day. Rather than guessing how much you will make, consider the following tips in order to find the right pricing for your apartment.

Keep The Pricing Low At The Start

In the last chapter, we talked a bit about titles of listings. If your title is attractive and if you promote your apartment as a cheap offer, there is a very good chance that your initial bookings will be very high. This is a great way to build your credibility in the market and get your host rating high. When you are new to Airbnb it will be very difficult to compete against other hosts that have thousands of reviews against their name. This is a great way to capture a lot of bookings and get a lot of positive reviews.

Don't Stay On The Low Pricing For Too Long

Once you have got a lot of positive reviews, you should gradually start increasing the prices to match the service that you provide. Although you may have a full booking and your occupancy rate is very high, you may lose out on profit margins if you continue at a low price for too long. While you may have 75% occupancy for the coming three or four weeks, you can gradually increase your prices and target higher profits for the future.

Change Your Prices According To The Day Of The Week

You may have noticed, hotels usually charge a very high price on weekends because that's when the demand is higher. This is the reason you need to differentiate between your prices for the week as compared to the weekend. If you are not sure what price you need to keep for the week and the weekend then you can look at your competitors in the area or you can look at the local hotels and see the prices they are offering.

Seasonal Pricing

Most properties usually lose out on making a high profit because they are not able to attract a lot of off season bookings. While most properties would have a high occupancy rate during peak season, attracting customers during off season is something that will set you apart. This is the reason you need to make sure that you implement seasonal pricing in order to attract guests during the off season too. If your prices are set too high during the off season, your occupancy rate will be affected and you will end up losing out on a lot of money.

Smart Pricing

Not a lot of hosts know this but Airbnb has a tool that all hosts can use. This tool ensures that the price will automatically change depending on the demand for the property. This facility is called smart pricing. When you switch on the smart pricing feature, the pricing will automatically adjust depending on the minimum and maximum price ranges that you have set for your property. This pricing will vary based on the supply and demand that is there for your particular location or specific dates. The pricing will also change depending on the amenities, the booking history, and the features that you are offering.

CHAPTER 7

Hosting Checklist

Once you complete your profile with Airbnb all you need to do is begin the listing and ensure that it manages to gather as much attention as possible so that you have reservations throughout. It can get really exciting and you may get eager to get your first reservation on Airbnb. Once you have registered on Airbnb, there are certain rules that come into play and one of the most important rules is to make sure that no matter how excited you get at getting your first booking, it should only be done through the platform. The last thing you want is for somebody to try and promise you a payment outside of Airbnb and then fail to pay.

Although the chances are slim, there are still a number of people out there who may promise that they will stay at your apartment and pay you the amount later on. It doesn't really work in your favor because most of these people never pay and since you haven't completed the transaction through Airbnb, it is not a secure transaction.

One cannot stress enough the importance of completing all transactions as well as ensuring that all communication takes place on the platform. Apart from focusing on only communicating with your guests through the Airbnb platform, you also need to make other preparations which include keeping the house ready for guests. There are various things that you can do in order to make your home comfortable but one of the best things is to keep it clean and make it an inviting setting for guests to come and stay. People look for warmth and comfort when they rent properties on Airbnb and the last thing you want to do is to end up creating a space that is empty and dull. Do not shy away from expressing the colors that you love or even adding a personal touch to the property. When you rent out your property, remember that people are coming to the area to explore it and learn more about it. So when you add a touch of culture to the property or even a room, it helps people connect with the area better.

Setting Of The House

When registering on Airbnb, make sure that the property or room that you plan on renting out is appealing to the eyes and up to the standards and requirements of your guests. Different people have different requirements but the one important thing that you need to remember is to provide them with the basic amenities that can ensure their comfort and encourage them to review your place in a positive way.

Your bed should have a soft comfortable mattress and the pillows should also be fluffy and soft. Also take into consideration that while some people like to use one pillow to sleep, there are others who may prefer using two or more pillows. So always stock up on pillows or cushions to ensure that the guests are comfortable. You should always keep a good amount of bed sheets and blankets in stock. Also, make sure that they are a little darker in shade because they tend to get stained less often and they look new. You should remember to replace the bed sheets and covers after every guest checks-out to maintain hygiene. You should also have good colored curtains to maintain privacy.

One of the best things to do when you set up a property for people to rent is to keep minimalist furniture in the house because then there is less risk of anything breaking or getting damaged. Televisions are highly recommended because it keeps guests entertained when they have nothing else to do. It may seem odd but a lot of guests still look for a television in the property because they tend to enjoy certain sports which they may not want to miss out on even while on vacation.

As a host you should also be open to the idea of subscribing to a new channel in case it's not in the package, just to increase credibility and make your guests as comfortable as possible. There are various subscriptions that you can choose from these days and these include Netflix or Amazon Prime. They are worth the investment because it has a lot to offer to people coming from different countries and they will definitely find something to keep them entertained. You may also want to consider stocking up the refrigerator with basic amenities. Cutlery and plates should also be stocked up because this encourages comfort and it allows guests to eat meals whenever they want. You could also choose to include a gas stove or an induction cooker and a microwave. While you do not have to invest in all of these amenities instantly, it is something that you should always have as a long term plan to keep your guests comfortable and provide them with the best service. When it comes to decorating the house you can always add a little personalized touch, such as a few showpieces or paintings to create a warm atmosphere. Refrain from dark-themed items and look for something that is peaceful yet cheerful.

You should also make sure you look for a toiletry supplier who can give you small bottles of shampoos, soaps, creams, and conditioners that you can replace for every guest. This works out really well because it helps you to save a lot of money that you would have invested in large bottles which you need to replace after each guest has moved out. Make sure you have a good number of towels that you can stock up in all the bathrooms and always have a separate pair that can be replaced once these go to the laundry. As a host, the most important thing you need to remember is that as soon as your guest checks out, you need to reset the house and keep it ready for the next guest to step in. A clean house is always warmer and receives better reviews in comparison to something that is even slightly dirty.

Cleaning The House

It is important for you to maintain cleanliness if you want to be an Airbnb host for a long time. One of the most important factors to take into consideration is getting the floors and the utensils cleaned on a regular basis. While cobweb cleaning is something that should be done weekly, the floors need to be cleaned every second day even when your guests are living in the apartment. You may want to get in touch with a cleaning person who can come into the apartment every second day to clean up the entire apartment. This includes your bathrooms and toilets as well. You could consider investing in a vacuum if it will make life easier. You should also advise the cleaner to clean up in a quick manner when there are guests inside the property but spend time cleaning every nook and corner once the guests checkout. You should have two kinds of cleaning services. One which is a basic clean and the other would be an advanced clean. The basic clean is something that applies to the caretaker when the guests are inside the property and the advance clean is something they should do once the guests vacate.

You should also advise your cleaners to make sure that the bathroom tiles are scrubbed after every guest vacates and the sink and bathtub are cleaned effectively. Sometimes your guests might stain the furniture or the carpet or even mess up the kitchen and this is something that needs to be taken into consideration when you sign up as an Airbnb host. This is why you should plan on renovating your kitchen and stick to darker colors. A smart thing to keep in mind is to not keep glass items around the house because they tend to break more easily. You can always choose plastic or microwave safe melamine which is less risky and will not break as easily. When guests stay at a rented property they do not look after cutlery and crockery as effectively as they do for their own so you may want to try and provide them with something that is durable and less fragile.

Fixing Hazards

When you become an Airbnb host there are various things that you need to take into consideration and one of them is issues that will come up with the property from time to time. One of them could be unclogging the sink or someone may break the shower or rip your shower curtain. The bulbs may blow or your air conditioning remote may need a change of batteries. All of these need to be taken into consideration and rectified as soon as possible. If your guest has complained about a persistent problem with the property, you need to send someone to the property as soon as possible to get it rectified without any further delay. The last thing you want is for your guests to stay in a property that has a problem as this will eventually get into the review.

In order for you to avoid this problem completely, individually check every little detail of the property and this includes the functionality of all the electrical appliances and the bulbs in the house. Make sure that all the remote controls are tested and the heating system in the house works efficiently. You should also check the television and make sure that the subscription is not nearing expiry so that you do not risk not providing a promised subscription service to the guests when they arrive.

It's important to regularly check on the mattress as well as the pillows that you have provided in case they have gone flat, you may want to consider giving them some sun so they fluff up again or you can replace them if they have grown too old. While you are renting out an apartment you may want to consider providing them with hotel quality mattresses because the comfort that they are seeking is usually dependent on the mattress that they sleep on. Always check the sofa bed to make sure that it opens and closes easily, check to see that it is clean as well.

Replacing Linens

As an Airbnb host, it could get a little daunting for you to constantly keep every nook and corner of the apartment clean and there will be times when you think that the apartment is clean and sparkling but your new guests do not think so and they look for a change. Even if the bed looks like no one has used it, if someone rents the apartment, even for a night, it is compulsory for you to replace the linens not only because it is ethical but also there are various infections that can transfer from one person to another. This is a precaution in case your previous guest had a contagious skin disease or something that could be transmitted through the linen. While this is rare, it is possible, and the last thing you want to do is take that risk because if a guest figures out that they contracted an infection because of linen that was not clean and wasn't changed, this could ruin your career as an Airbnb host permanently. Hygiene is something that needs to be given utmost importance and this is why you have to ensure that you have a lot of spare bed sheets and towels available so you can constantly rotate and replace them even when you send one to the laundry. If you plan on steaming the carpet, you may want to send in the cleaner and get all of the carpets and cushions steamed in a single day. Sometimes guests get paranoid and may ask for a replacement every second day and while this may seem a little too demanding, you need to make sure that you keep them as comfortable as possible if you want that good review. This is why you need to agree to the requests, even if it sounds unreasonable at times.

Empty The Refrigerator

We have already spoken about the importance of having a clean house and making sure that your cleaner takes out all the dirt before the new guests arrive. Checking the refrigerator should also be a mandatory process on the checklist for your cleaner every time they enter the house to do a thorough cleaning before new guests arrive. The reason it is so important for your cleaner to clean the refrigerator regularly is because guests are usually messy and they tend to keep leftover food in the fridge that they often forget about. This could also include a packet of leftover biscuits or even a half-eaten pizza that could create a stench in the refrigerator, if not cleaned.

During the cleaning process, you should also make sure that your cleaner stocks up the refrigerator with a carton of milk, eggs, and some fruit. This is necessary because it helps your guests to have a basic breakfast once they arrive and it makes them feel good.

A lot of Airbnb hosts decide not to keep food in the house because they need to constantly restock and this could eat into their profits, but the truth is that when you go the extra mile you make your guest feel more welcome and that's the difference between a hotel stay and staying at an Airbnb house, which is something everybody looks forward to doing.

Secure Your Valuables

A lot of people who stay at an Airbnb are curious and this means that they will open up every door inside the house to see what is inside of it. If you are renting out your old apartment or a place that you lived in previously, the last thing you want is to have any personal items in that house such as photographs of your family. Do not try to associate the flat with you by leaving around things that represent your family or even anything that has religious context because you don't really know what kind of people will be staying in your house. You may also want to ensure that all the items in the property are durable and unbreakable as much as possible because guests do not really look after your valuables as well as you would look after them. Do not keep any jewelry or financial documents, it's best to remove them before you decide to become an Airbnb host. The reason it is important to have surveillance in the common areas is this keeps your valuables safe and secure. Surveillance will ensure that nobody is just going to walk out of the room taking your microwave or your television along with them.

Make An Extra Guest Key

It is important to have at least three copies of the key to the property at any given time because this makes it convenient for you to handle the reservations even when you have multiple locations to deal with. You should always leave spare keys with the cleaner or the caretaker of the house and one set of keys should be with you. When a guest rents the property, one of the sets of keys goes to the guest while they stay at the property and the second set still remains with the caretaker. You need to remember that the minute your guest goes, you may want to change the lock in case the guest made a copy of the key. You also need to remember that if your keys have been lost multiple times, you may want to consider changing the locks as well.

There are going to be a ton of tips and tricks available for you to follow when it comes to becoming an excellent Airbnb host; however at the end of the day, these practices go a long way. This guide will help you understand how to become an Airbnb host and help you to understand the different things that you need to take into consideration. There will be ups and downs that you will face and there will be a number of hiccups along the way, but you need to find the perfect solution to work around it and make sure that you do not stop working towards making yourself a better host. A wise man once said that if you are not successful tomorrow it's because you didn't work hard enough for it today. As an Airbnb host, you need to make sure that you work as hard as possible to provide every guest who comes to stay in your apartment with the comfort and warmth that they are seeking.

CHAPTER 8

Tips & Tricks For The Host

As an Airbnb host, there are a number of things that you need to do that will help improve the experience of the guests that are staying in your property. If you want great reviews on the platform then you will need to make sure that you make your guests feel special and pampered. While it may not be possible to personally interact with the guests at all times, you will need to make sure that there is some level of personalization with them so that they feel welcome and they do not get the feeling of living in a hotel room. If being an Airbnb host is not the only job that you do then there is a possibility that you will be away from home during your working hours. Here are a few tips that will help up you get better reviews on Airbnb and make your guests feel special.

Doing Something Different

The level of interaction you have with the guests will also influence a lot of other travelers that are looking to rent your property. Travelers usually look at the reviews and see what the previous guests have to say about their interaction with you. In order to earn extra profit through Airbnb, offer a few extra services, especially when you start up. Go the extra mile in order to make sure that your guests feel welcome and they leave a five-star rating for you after each and every stay. Reading what other guests are saying about your competitors and reading the reviews that they are leaving can give you valuable insight. You will start noticing that the host that goes the extra mile is appreciated a lot more.

Make Sure That Your Guest Does Not Wait

If your apartment is in a major city then there is a very good chance that your guest will arrive at very odd hours. Get ready to greet your guest, no matter what time of the day or night it is. If your work timing does not permit you to meet your guests personally, then have a family member or a friend there to greet them. Greeting guests is something that makes a guest feel extra special and that is the reason someone should be present in your apartment, irrespective of the arrival time. If your guest has to wait for you at the airport or the local railway station for hours, imagine the reviews that you will receive after they have completed their stay with you.

Pick Up Facility

Most travelers in a major city look for extra facilities when booking a property. While most hotels would provide an airport pickup and drop, you could do the same as an Airbnb host. This will create a great first impression if you are available to greet your guests at the train station or at the airport. Guests usually do not like looking for the house in a new city. If you are unable to pick them up yourself, make sure that you take care of their pick up or provide accurate instructions with regards to transportation.

Help Them Get Around

Most people that book stays with Airbnb usually visit the city for tourism purposes. One of the best things that you can do is create a welcome package for all your guests. This welcome package can contain information that they may find helpful when they are staying in the city. This package should include your contact details, names, and addresses of a few local restaurants and other tourism places or activities that are happening in your area. When you check back with them the next day, ask them if they need anything else and if their first day was fine. If you are open to socializing you could even offer to spend some time with your guests or accompany them to a few places if they are fine with it.

Be Different From The Others

Almost every Airbnb host offers the same kind of services and amenities to their guests. You can differentiate yourself from these hosts and offer something extra to your guests. This could be in the form of a free meal at a local restaurant, a box of homemade cupcakes, or even a free ride to a major tourist attraction. Guests will look at the effort that you are making and the popularity of the listing spreads through word of mouth.

Ask Your Guest For References

The beginning of your journey as an Airbnb host can be extremely rough. If you are new to the world of Airbnb, you may find it a bit difficult to get your first guest. Travelers very rarely look for places that don't have reviews. Once you get your first guest, you then need to make sure that you ask them to refer family members and friends to your property. If you have not received your first guest within the first month, you can ask your own friends or family members to write references for you. They can write reviews as if they have stayed at your apartment and this will help other travelers understand the kind of experience you are offering.

CHAPTER 9

Handling A Bad Review On Airbnb

Being part of Airbnb is all about being a part of the service industry. Every host has to make sure that the guest is as comfortable as possible and they will want repeat business from these customers. Another thing that hosts usually look for are references from their current customers so that their business can grow. The one thing that will stop hosts from receiving repeat business or new business is through bad reviews. Bad reviews or negative reviews are the one thing that all Airbnb hosts fear. The impact a negative review has on the apartment listing is beyond compare. A number of hosts have been forced to shut down the listing when they received a couple of bad reviews because they know it is difficult to bounce back from these reviews. However, these reviews are simple to deal with and you can convert bad reviews into a positive review for your business. With this chapter, you will learn how to deal with negative reviews as a host and how to convert bad reviews into something positive that will help your property listing.

Learn The Truth

As an Airbnb host, you will not receive a five-star rating from all your guests. There are a few things that will always irk a customer and it's important to understand the truth behind the reviews before you go about reacting to one. Here are a few things to be aware of before you start reacting to bad reviews. These are:

- A bad review can actually help your business grow.

- Just because you received a negative review does not mean that your property is bad.

- You can handle a bad review with ease.

Now let us look at the ways to combat bad reviews and how to make sure that it does not affect your Airbnb listing.

Believe In Your Apartment

Just because you received a bad review does not mean that your apartment is bad. It's very easy to start believing reviews that you've received and start doubting your Airbnb listing. Yes, maybe you received a bad review and maybe something went wrong but that does not mean that it is the end of the world. It means that there are certain things that you can do differently in order to change the opinion of your guests. As an Airbnb host, you will come across a couple of bad reviews every once in a while. If your property is extremely popular and there are guests occupying it 90% to 95% of the time, then there is a chance that you will receive bad reviews once or twice a month. Not every product that receives a bad review needs to be taken off the shelf. Similarly not every property that receives a bad review needs to go off Airbnb. The first thing to do when you receive a bad review is to remind yourself that your property is up to the required standards. If there is something that is truly bad about your property such as a leakage problem or maybe an insect infestation then it is your responsibility to get rid of those problems. However, if there are no such obvious problems in your house then you need to believe that your property is perfect as it is.

The Bad Reviews Help Your Good Reviews

This may sound odd but when there are a couple of bad reviews followed by a handful of good reviews, it will put you in a good light. Your prospective travelers will see that you are making an effort to convert your bad reviews into good reviews. If your bad reviews continue to stay the same and the same feedback is received every now and then, that is when people will start doubting your property listing and they will not book your property. However, if there is a bad review that speaks about your attitude and there are a couple of good reviews after it that speak about you being very helpful and friendly then the next traveler will see that. All people want to see is an improvement. They do not want to see bad reviews over and over again and if this happens it would probably mean that you will need to cancel your Airbnb listing. You need to start working on the feedback that you receive so that the next review will reflect very nicely on your attitude.

Another good thing about bad reviews is it makes your listing look authentic. How many times have you looked at a product online and asked yourself 'how come there are no bad reviews for the product'? When a product has five-star reviews consistently for a couple of years it will start looking unauthentic. People do not believe that every product or brand is flawless. That is the reason your bad review will actually reflect well on your listing and people will know that your property is worth renting.

Change The Expectations

A bad review usually reflects on the expectations vs reality aspect. This means that your guests had certain expectations from you or from your property and those expectations were not met. What this simply means is you should make sure that you are matching your guests' expectations with the reality. This is where your property listing comes into the picture. When you promise too much and deliver little, people will start getting disappointed in the service that is provided to them. When you want a property with a pool and you pay a certain amount for it and the pool is not available to you during that time, you are bound to be upset as a customer. Although the property may be flawless, that one promise that was not fulfilled can result in a bad review. This is the reason you need to make sure that you correctly setout the expectations in your listing and you meet those expectations to the best of your ability.

Dealing With Bad Reviews

There are a few simple ways that you can deal with bad reviews, but keep in mind that you must deal with them as soon as possible. Letting a review stay online without an explanation or a justification from you can have adverse effects on your listing. Here are a few steps that you need to take when you are responding to a bad review.

Don't Panic

It is very easy to hit the panic button when a bad review is posted about your property listing. If you are new to the world of Airbnb hosting then you have all the more reason to panic and start doubting your capabilities as a host. There have been people that have functioned efficiently as an Airbnb host despite receiving a bad review as their very first review. Receiving a bad review is not the end of the world and as we stated above it can actually help your business in a number of ways.

Never Remove Bad Reviews

Another temptation that you will have when you receive bad reviews is to delete the reviews. You should always resist the temptation to remove these reviews because it will not reflect well on your ethics. There will be a lot of unhappy customers if you do not meet people's expectations. But hiding your reviews is not something that you need to do. You need to make sure that you publish your negative reviews along with your positive reviews and this will make people trust you even more. When you start deleting negative reviews, the travelers that have actually stayed and left those reviews will start noticing that you are deleting these reviews. They will then find another way to get the reviews across and that will bring you down even more drastically.

Respond Publicly And Quickly

Responding to a negative review is never easy. There are a number of emotions involved but it is a matter of protecting your listing. When you are responding to a negative review there are a few things to keep in mind. First and foremost you need to ensure that you care about what is written in the review. It is very easy to brush off the review and respond back in a negative way. When you start acknowledging bad reviews and you show the person that you care, it will reflect well and people will start saying that you have a positive frame of mind. You should also resolve negative reviews publicly by posting positive responses. People will always pay attention to all the mistakes that you made and the problems that are related to your listing. Once they read all that has been posted regarding the property, they will then check the resolution that the people have received. When they see that a resolution has been provided, they will not hesitate to rent your apartment for their next trip. When you start responding to negative reviews publicly and you provide apt resolutions, there is a very good chance that there will be a significant increase in your occupancy rate.

Learn From Your Reviews

Being an Airbnb host is never easy. There are a number of things that you need to take care of as a host and these are the lessons that you learn as you go forward on the journey. While you may have people around to assist you or to give you advice, the feedback that you receive from your reviews can also teach you a lot. It is not only negative feedback that can teach you but there are some words of wisdom in positive reviews as well. Make sure that you address all the core issues that are mentioned in the negative reviews and respond back in a timely manner. This could be small things such as the guest not liking the photograph type you posted about the apartment or maybe the address not being very clear. When you promise a guest that certain things would be taken care of, you need to make sure that you take care of these things so that next time they will want to come back and rent your property again. No matter how small the feedback is, you need to show your guests that you value their feedback and you act upon the feedback as soon as possible.

Follow Up

Providing a resolution to a review may seem to be extremely easy but following up on that resolution is a tough commitment. When a guest states that he or she did not like your property listing or they did not like certain curtains that were put up in the house, then act upon that review and follow up with the customer to see if they liked your action. Trust me, your guest will be very impressed when they see the kind of commitment you have towards their review. When you start following up on all of your actions, you will soon see that your negative reviews are turning into positive and promotional reviews. Word of mouth publicity is the best way to get your property up to 100% occupancy. This can only be done with your hard work and commitment.

Combating Negative Reviews

Before you go about combating negative reviews you should

also look at the good reviews that you have received. If your good reviews are not that high then you need to start focusing on getting more good reviews and this can be done in 3 very simple ways. Let us look at how you can get more good reviews so that your negative reviews are negated.

Mobile Friendly Reviews

Most of the people that use Airbnb use it on their mobile phones. It is very rare for a person to use a computer to visit the Airbnb website to browse through listings or to book a property. When you do not make the review process friendly for mobile users, you will not receive that many reviews. This means that if you receive a couple of negative reviews and very few good reviews, the negative reviews will stand out in the review section. When you make the review section mobile friendly, you will encourage more and more people to give reviews for your listing. This means that there is a better chance of you receiving positive reviews on your listing. People are always on the go and they have very little time to sit in front of a desktop or laptop to leave a review for an Airbnb listing. However, if they are able to provide a review through their smartphone then they will be more than happy to do so while they are traveling or during their break. When you collect a lot of positive reviews you will be able to negate the bad reviews that you received.

Offering Incentives

It is very rare for an Airbnb host to repay guests when they leave a review. However, it doesn't mean that it cannot be done. You can offer incentives to your customers for every positive review that they leave for you. This could be in the form of a discount on the next booking or it could also be in the form of freebies when they stay with you the next time around. Irrespective of what you offer, you need to make sure that you live up to the commitment because people will expect these freebies when they leave positive reviews for you. When you start offering incentives, you will see that the number of reviews have gone up and this will help with sweeping the negative reviews off your listing page.

Ask For Reviews

If you are not able to afford to give out freebies to your customers for providing positive reviews, you can blatantly ask your guests for it. There is no shame in asking for a review from your guests and it will only make them feel valued because you are valuing their feedback. When your guests are leaving your apartment, you can leave them a small thank you note and ask them to leave a positive review if they enjoyed their stay. In this way, you will receive reviews for every stay that has been completed in your property and there is a very good chance that these reviews will also be positive.

CHAPTER 10

Key Exchange

When you become an Airbnb host the most important job to get done as seamlessly as possible is handing over the key to the guest. When you start out, it's not easy for you to hire a cleaning service to look after the needs of the property and this means that small tasks such as handing over the key become your responsibility. This is the first ever contact with the guest that you will have and it is essential for you to make it as pleasant as possible so that the guest feels happy as soon as they step into the property. Remember that just because the guest has the key, doesn't mean that your job is done. This is because you will want a positive review and the only way they will do this is when you provide them with the warm and welcoming stay that they have been looking forward to. When you treat your guests well there is a strong chance that they will leave a positive review for you and this will definitely work out well for you. Find the most effective way for you to hand over the key to the guest because you do not want any chaos to be there just as the guest is checking in. Depending on what situation you are in, there are various solutions that you can find for the problem. So let's take a look at some of the best alternatives for you to hand over your key to the guest in case you are not around.

Asking A Friend Or Family Member To Hand Over The Key

Being an Airbnb host doesn't necessarily mean that you have to give up your day job. In such a scenario, it could get a little difficult for you to handle a booking and ensure that you have made it to your job at the same time. In case you plan to hold onto your 9 to 5 job and a guest is coming in a little later during the day, then you can always ask your family members to help you with handing over the keys or else you could even ask a friend of yours to do it for you.

When you ask somebody to hand over the keys, you need to make sure that the person handing over the keys is responsible and won't delay the exchange in any way. The guests who are coming to stay at your place will be tired from their trip and the last thing they want is to wait a long time before they can enter the property that they've rented. You also need to make sure that the guest is aware of who will be handing over the keys to them. Give your guests the keyholder's contact number so that they can stay in touch with them from when they arrive until they reach the location. In case nobody is around for you to handle this exchange then you can always request your neighbor to do it for you. If a neighbor is available and there is a large family arriving, it makes it that much easier for you because you know for a fact that someone will always be at home to provide the guest with the key. However, when you give the keys to your neighbor you need to make sure that you call your neighbor and ask them whether or not they will be around the tentative time when you think the guests will be arriving. When providing your neighbors with a tentative time, try to provide them with a window that is a little larger than the window that your guest has provided.

Dropping At A Nearby Shop

If there is nobody available for you to handle the exchange from your family or friends circle, and you don't really know your neighbors well, then you could consider handing it over to a nearby shop as long as you trust them. A number of Airbnb hosts tend to rent out their old apartments. This means that they have stayed in that apartment for a relatively long time and they are well connected with the people around the area, including the shopkeepers. If there is a cafe or a coffee shop around then it makes a lot of sense to drop off the keys at the shop because a coffee shop is usually open 7 days a week and this makes it convenient for your guests to pick up the keys when they arrive.

This is a great resolution as long as you trust the person handling the keys and you know for a fact that they will be responsible as well as attentive to the guests who come to pick up the key. As a goodwill gesture, you may also want to purchase coffee for the guests so that the shopkeeper feels good about helping you since they also manage to get business out of you. When you decide to drop off the keys at a nearby shop you may also want to consider the arrival time of your guests because if they arrive during work hours then it's great and convenient for your guest to pick up the keys from the nearby shop; but if they are arriving at odd hours then you may need to think of an alternative.

Using An External Service

When you just start out as an Airbnb host you may not be able to afford a full-time caretaker which is why you may want to consider external services. These are people who are available and work on a commission basis. This is simple and all you need to do is get in touch with the agency that can provide you with this service whenever you need them to be available. Not only do they handle the keys for your property, they also offer other services such as sightseeing tours or flight tickets. If you are busy with work and you still want to make time to be an Airbnb host, then hiring external services makes a lot of sense because this person will look after your guest whenever there is any help needed. In case your guests need constant guidance with regards to where they need to go from time to time or with instructions or direction, then you are always going to benefit from an external service because you know that the person will help them get the information that they need.

Key Box

A key box is a small security device that is available for people to use when they are not around and they still want to share a set of keys with a guest. This box basically has a four-digit code that needs to be entered in order for the guest to get the keys and all you need to do is provide the guest with this code once they have arrived. This key box can be fitted on the main door or in a secret spot so that the guest can operate it when they get there.

The digital lock can be controlled by a four-digit code or by a mobile device, depending on what you want to provide the guest with.

If you are just starting out as an Airbnb host, then cutting down your expenses may be your number one priority but you need to remember that providing guests with effective service is also necessary because if you don't, then you won't be in the business long enough to make the most out of the hosting service you are providing.

CHAPTER 11

Becoming A Superhost On Airbnb

Some guests come in early and leave late and as a host, it gets really difficult for you to decide whether or not you need to lay down certain rules or are ready to bend your rules based on the requirements of your guest. A lot of Airbnb guests believe that they are ready to be as flexible as possible and bend the rules for their guest just so that they get a positive review but this may not be the most convenient thing for to you to do because, at the end of the day, it is your property and without rules it is going to be difficult for you to control the behavior of the guest.

A responsible Airbnb host should have a list of house rules that are not that rigid but also manage to draw the line just right so that nothing gets out of hand and you do not get in trouble with the law. You have to remember that anyone who stays in your property becomes your responsibility and if anything goes wrong, you will be the one who will have to face the music and the last thing you want is to create problems for yourself. While it seems very difficult to set house rules for your guests, this is something you should pay a lot of attention to and take time to draft. You will find a lot of resolutions and solutions on the internet as well and you can go through the various competitor's house rules to see what they've decided to allow or disallow on their property. Make a list of the things that you think you should include and start following them accordingly. There are different house rules for different cities and countries but some rules remain generic and are the same to people all across the world. Let's take a look at some of the house rules that you should decide whether you want to set or not.

Remember, the rules you set at the house are something that the guest will also read, so it's important to include everything in the rules and not miss out on even the smallest detail. During the time of booking, you should always confirm with the guest whether or not they agree with the rules just so you know that the guest and you are on the same page. It is common for a guest to see a listing and show interest without actually seeing what the rules state and what the Airbnb host has to say about certain rules. Here are a few categories that you should consider when it comes to the rules of the house.

Extra Guest

On your Airbnb listing you should always provide the maximum number of guests that you are ready to accommodate on the property and this will usually include the space available in the bedroom and in the living area. If you have space for five people in your property, you may want to list the apartment as a space for only four people. This is mainly because you should provide guests with extra space and not make the house too overcrowded. Even if you have extra sleeping space, listing the apartment with one less count is always better because when a person looks for space to rent, they tend to look for one or two over or below the limit. If you are ready to provide your guests with a sleeping mattress that they can put on the floor, and if they are fine with this then you should decide whether you are going to permit extra guests to stay in the propery and if you are going to permit them, then how much will you charge for the extra guest.

Some Airbnb hosts decide not to charge for extra guests but this is something that you should always charge for because you need to stock supplies in the house based on the number of guests that you are expecting. For example, if there are five people staying in the house then you know that you need to keep five towels and five pillows for them but if there is going to be an extra guest then you need to increase the number in stock and this also includes any food that you provide.

When you provide space for an extra guest on your Airbnb listing, you not only need to take into consideration the bedding that you have, but you also have to arrange for the extra dishes and cutlery. Most people do not like to share towels, so you may want to provide one towel and one hand towel for guests and this will end up increasing your laundry charges. This is the reason you need to add all of that to the total amount that you will charge your guests. The best way to charge people for your listing is to have basic rent for the property and then a charge per person which will automatically increase as soon as the guest increases the number of people that will accompany them on the trip. This is a common practice and it is very convenient so you should make the most out of this and have a certain budget set aside for a person and make sure that the price increases as the number of heads increase.

Smoking

Whether or not you permit smoking inside your Airbnb property is completely your decision. However, keep in mind that when somebody smokes inside a confined space, it tends to linger for a long time and it will affect the smell of the rooms and various other items that are present in the house, including your clothes, linens, mattress, and pillow. There are also a number of smokers who feel a strong urge to smoke and this is why they choose to avoid hotel reservations. If you would like to stop the guest from smoking everywhere then you may want to consider informing them about a certain space in your house or a balcony where they could go and smoke.

If you want to allow your guest to smoke in a confined area then make sure that you make the area comfortable. This could mean providing a patio table and a chair or other furniture item as well as an ashtray so they know for a fact that this is the smoking area. If you want to make sure that the living room and the spaces that do not have too much ventilation are off-limits for smoking, then inform guests before they check in and make it clear to them that if they do smoke in the area that is restricted for smoking, they will be fined.

Eating

Your guests will eat inside your property and you can't stop them from doing so but you can definitely have spaces where you restrict them from eating or you could label those areas 'food free zones'. This could be the bedrooms so that you protect your bed and you ensure that there are no ants or other such problems. The best way to control people's eating habits and try to confine them to a certain area to eat is to have a dining table arranged. If you provide them with a space to eat their food there is a strong chance that they will eat in the area that is provided for them to eat and they will not mess up the entire house. These are the rules you need to make clear with them and you should also mention that if they stain your linens they will be fined. Some of these rules may seem to be a little harsh but if you want to stay in business for the long-term and you want to maintain the quality of your property, you need to put certain restrictions on people because some people will not look after your property unless they are pressured into doing so.

Cleaning

When your guests stay in your property for more than a day there is going to be a lot of garbage that gets accumulated and you have to set rules with regards to how they will sort out the trash. Many countries follow dry and wet garbage disposal system and the rules for this disposal system may differ from country to country. If you follow this rule and you want to make sure that recycling is a part of your Airbnb hosting program then you should inform your guests in advance what waste material goes into which bag and where they need to place the bins. A simple color code works well for most guests and you should always try to inform them about how it works as well.

When your guests use your utensils to cook, it's not going to be possible for your cleaning person to clean on a regular basis and if the guests would like to clean up after their meals, then provide them with cleaning agents like dish washing detergent and a scrubber. You should also mention where these items are placed in case they are away from sight and you could also inform the guests that they should not leave any utensils in the basin.

Laundry

Some Airbnb apartments come with a washer and a dryer and allow guest to use them. Some apartments have a common laundry area that they can visit for a small fee. In case you have a common laundry area, you may want to inform the guest with regards to the charges and the operation of the space. It is important for you to keep your guest as informed as possible because a lot of times, your guests are the harshest critics and they may get upset at something that wasn't even part of your initial plan as a host. While you do not expect your guests to wash your bed sheets and towels they may want to clean up their own clothes or may even want to clean the towels more regularly than you replace them and in this situation, the best thing to do is to provide them with an alternative for laundry services. In case there is no washer and dryer available in your property and there is no laundry in the building, you can always give them the address to a laundromat that is close by. This is something that comes in handy, especially for guests staying for a prolonged period.

Gatherings Or Parties

Sometimes you will come across guests who request to have

parties in your property and they may even want permission to allow extra people who will not sleep over for the night. Making a call with regards to whether or not you want to allow this gathering and if you want to prevent them at all cost is dependent on you.

If your property is secluded and there are no neighboring houses that will get disturbed with loud music and a large number of people gathered together then you can consider providing your space for parties and social gatherings; however if you have neighbors who may get disturbed by the noise, this is something you should think about before you allow it. Parties and social gatherings, especially when in somebody else's house, can tend to get a little noisy and there is a higher risk of things getting broken, dirty, and spoilt. So take your time to think about the items present in your house and whether or not they are safe from large gatherings. If you have the space to accommodate people you still need to make a decision with regards to whether or not you are fine with having so many people in the property at the same time. Also take into consideration the laws regarding the gathering of crowds and if your state falls under laws where you cannot have a certain number of people present together on a rental property, you may want to reconsider parties and gatherings.

Alcohol And Drugs

There are lots of guests that discuss alcohol and drugs with their Airbnb host but it is your responsibility to make it clear to your guest, whether or not you are comfortable with them drinking alcohol or not. While drugs are something that you should have strict rules about regardless, alcohol can always be considered. If your guests are young, you can ask them to provide you with their ID proof with regards to their age, as well as their permanent address just so that you know how old the people staying in your property are. If there are people who are slightly underage and may not be permitted by the law to drink, you may want to hold back on giving them permission to drink because the last thing you want is for them to do something stupid while in your property. Alcohol and drugs could get the better of any person and they may not think as rationally as they should which is why prohibiting the consumption of alcohol and drugs is highly recommended for an Airbnb host.

Quiet Hours

If you are renting out a property that has a lot of houses in close proximity to it then you have to take into consideration your neighbors' comfort as well. Provide your guests with certain rules that prohibit them from playing loud music or talking or screaming too loudly at certain hours because this disturbs the peace of everybody surrounding the house and it could create problems for you as an Airbnb host.

In case there are schools that are in close proximity to the property, you have to make sure that you mention this in the rules and you also keep it clear that it should not be noisy because it will disturb the students studying there. As an Airbnb host you should try to be as considerate as possible with everybody in your surrounding area because the more considerate you are, the less likely you are to get into a dispute with someone.

If you want to grow as a host, you have to compromise in certain areas and also put your foot down with guests if you do not agree with them on certain decisions. Most Airbnb guests understand the house rules that are set by the host but in case they do not, you may want to be a little strict with them and if somebody complains about the behavior of your guest, you must address the guest and ask them not to do that again. Just because you are scared about getting rated badly on Airbnb, you should not allow your guest to do anything that they want to because that will have long term effects on your hosting services with Airbnb.

Children

Some Airbnb hosts take it very lightly when it comes to families that come with children and they believe that since they are accompanied by elders, the children are not your responsibility. As an Airbnb host, you have to be just as responsible as the parents are when renting out a property and in case you know that your home is not suitable for children, you may want to put that in your notes. Houses that do not have a grill to protect a window or have open spaces that a child can jump from should not be rented to families that have small children. If you have a house that is baby friendly, this may be something that you may want to highlight in your listing and it should also include photographs of the space that is child-friendly. This could include a crib, a high seat for a baby, and other things that make the house baby proof.

Remember, when it comes to something happening to children while staying at your property this is an issue for you as a host not only because of a low rating but also because Airbnb will start taking serious action against any complaint received from that child's parent against your property. You need to provide guests with a comfortable space and honest feedback with regards to what you have and what you do not have in the house. If it's not meant for babies, do not allow families with babies to come and stay because you don't want something to go wrong.

Pets

Pet-friendly hotels and resorts around the world are on the rise and a number of Airbnb hosts are also opening up to the idea of families with pets coming and staying in their home. Whether or not you like pets and whether you want them to come and stay in your property is something you need to decide in advance. Pets may seem like a big nuisance but actually, most are not and this gives you a wider market to cover as long as you are comfortable with the idea. Most families that travel with pets will include either cats or dogs, both of which can be trained and do not create too much chaos when they are in a new space. You may want to have certain rules with regards to whether you want to charge extra for the pet and you may also want to limit the areas where the pet is allowed to visit. For example, you may want to tell your guests that the pet shouldn't be allowed on the bed.

As a goodwill gesture, you can also keep a dog bed that is large enough to accommodate a large dog so that you don't have to worry about replacing the bed every time you have a new reservation. When there is a family that comes to stay without a pet, you should get rid of all the pet things but when a family with a pet comes along, you can bring all these items back. Remember that if you plan on keeping your home pet-friendly, invest in a strong vacuum cleaner and a lot of air fresheners. Pet owners love to say that pets are clean however that is not always the case, and when it comes to shedding and dander, it could be a problem for certain guests. This is why you need to keep your solutions ready for pet owners as well. There are a number of vacuum cleaners that specialize in getting rid of pet hair and there are also cleaning agents available that get rid of the slightest smell of a pet. You should invest in these if you plan on making your property pet-friendly.

CHAPTER 12

Alternative Methods To Promote Your Listing

Creating a profile on Airbnb and listing your property may seem easy when you follow a step-by-step procedure, however, it can be a little difficult, especially when there is a lot of competition in your area. While back in the day not too many people were aware of Airbnb and the benefits that it has to offer a host, today it's a different story and there are a lot of people who are inclined towards hosting on Airbnb because it's simple and effective. This is a good thing and it increases the competition for you. Whenever you plan to host on Airbnb, start thinking of innovative strategies for you to market your listing and make sure that you stand out from the crowd.

Now that you have your Airbnb listing set up and you have arranged for everything that is mentioned in this book so far, you are probably wondering what next? Well if you want to be a strong Airbnb host then you need to look at some subtle but interesting marketing techniques to secure your Airbnb listing. Take a look at some of these techniques that you can apply to your listing.

Create A Story To Support Your Listing

Everyone loves an amazing story and the fact that you are sharing one is something that is definitely going to drive a lot of attention to your listing. With amazing technology advancements and the tools available on your smartphone, you can create an interesting and engaging video that can help people learn more about the property that you are renting out and the reason behind it.

You don't have to spend a lot of money to create this video. All you need is to get some interesting photographs of the location, the interior of the house, and the places that people can visit once they rent your property. You can also highlight your unique selling point or USP in the story so that it grabs people's attention. While every Airbnb host has something different and unique about their property, it may not necessarily be noticed in the listing. When you put up a story, it allows people to get to know more about your property and the uniqueness of it. When travelers look at the story, it lets them know more about the experience you have as a host. This story can be shared on social media and you can even ask your friends to share it. When people travel from other cities or countries they usually have a lot of friends and if your story goes viral there is a strong chance that they may recommend your Airbnb listing for them to rent. Good news travels fast and there is no better place for you to share news than on social media, so make sure that you make a story that goes viral and creates waves so that people learn about you as a host and the place that you are renting out.

When you create your story, you may also want to consider targeting pages on social media that are relevant to the experience you provide. If there is a trail that's popular near your property, try to highlight it and inform people about the various benefits of coming and staying at your property and how they can get the most out of the trek. You can even go as far as to get contact numbers of people who organize treks from time to time and co-ordinate to provide them with people to participate in the trek. The more involved you are with your listing, the higher the chances of you getting people to stay and rent your property.

Get In Touch With A Lifestyle Blogger Or A Journalist

You may be able to create a video that can talk about your experience as an Airbnb host and your journey but when it comes to putting it out there, you may not be the best person to do it and that's where a blogger or a journalist comes in handy. Not only does a blogger help to create a really good storyline that you can share with the video but they also have a lot of followers who will check out the story when they share it. Most bloggers who have a following are also called influencers. This means they charge you a little money to post your story but it is worth spending that money because it can get you a lot of attention and once you get popular, there is no turning back. Making the right decisions can help you to become a superhost in no time and once you reach the position of a super host, there is nothing that will stop you.

However, if you don't have the budget to spend on these services, there are always other ways to look at it. You can look for journalists or bloggers that are looking for accommodation in your city and allow them to stay at your property for free. In return, you can ask them to write a short review and promote your property in some way. It's a great way to kick start your Airbnb career and while you may not earn from the rental, you will definitely get a lot of credit and this will help you start your Airbnb listing in a positive way.

Create A Unique URL

A lot of Airbnb hosts have a separate URL that helps them to promote the property that they have listed on Airbnb and while you may not consider doing this, it's definitely beneficial because it is easier to share that link with people than to share a link for the Airbnb listing, which could get daunting. Airbnb does not offer you a customized link option. So the best way for you to do it would be to use your own. When you create your own link you may want to highlight some of the best things about your property, this could include anything from the actual location or a nearby popular tourist spot that is well known across the world. When using your own domain try to get a '.com' as it is the easiest domain to remember and it is also convenient to visit. When promoting your Airbnb listing, try to promote your website rather than the actual listing and you can always use your website to redirect visitors to the actual listing where they can make their booking. Promoting an extremely long URL could get very difficult and certain platforms do not allow you to use characters beyond a certain limit. This will make it difficult for you to paste the entire URL. If you are not comfortable spending money on a domain or there's nothing unique about the property then you can always use a shortened URL to cut down the size so it will be easier to share. There are better chances of a small URL being clicked on in comparison to a larger one, so keep the URL as short as possible.

Join Vacation Rental Forums

Forums may seem old school and something hat not a lot of people use these days but they are just as popular as they were when they were first introduced into the market. When it comes to back and forth discussions with customers or potential customers, or finding the right solution to a problem, there's nothing better than a forum and if you're looking to grab people before they even reach the Airbnb app, joining a vacation rental forum is the best place for you to market. You can share pictures or the link for your listing and let people know why your place is worth renting. If you have just started out you may want to hit the forum and start off at a lower price in comparison to your competitors. This will help you get an edge over them and grab the audience as your customer before they even think about checking another listing. This may come as a surprise but 80% of people who look for properties on Airbnb compare the prices before they actually check the amenities and the area where they are looking for the property. So always remember to have your property listed at a lower rate when you have just started out. This gets you the kind of exposure you are seeking and when you treat your guest's right, it will give you positive feedback that eventually turns your place into a hot favorite for people on Airbnb. If you want to work your way up the ladder, you may want to consider lowering the budget a little bit so that you can get those customers. You will be surprised to see how much can change even with a $10 difference.

When it comes to being present on this forum you need to stay as active as possible so post every day so people know your listing exists. This is also a great place for you to get referrals and new customers to come to stay at your property.

Get Listed With Tourism Websites

There are various websites that talk about hotels, hostels, and homestays on their pages and if you come across websites that cater to your area, you can ask them to list your property on their site as well. While most of these websites will do it for free, they may ask you for a profit share or a small fee for every booking that comes through them. This is the reason you should always offer them some money because when you ask them to do this for free there is not a lot of motivation and they don't really focus too much on your listing but when you offer them money in return, they are always going to look to make that extra money by helping you rent out your property.

When you are listing your property with these websites always remember to keep the rate the same and ask them to book via the Airbnb website. While you may be spending a little more than you intended to on this reservation, it is better than having your property empty and not making any money at all.

Go Back To Traditional Advertising Techniques

Airbnb is a virtual platform where people can book a home in a city without being physically present in said city. This is why people tend to forget the importance of traditional marketing techniques like a newspaper advertisement or a flyer. Flyers are great because you can just leave them at a popular tourist destination and hope people get back to you from there. There might be a pin board in a restaurant or cafe where you can put up your Airbnb listing. Make sure that you do that even if they ask you for a small fee to allow you to put up your listing. You will be surprised to see how many people are not happy with the service they are getting at a hotel or another location and they are looking for new accommodation almost instantly. Sometimes people may be at the end of their stay and they may be looking for a new place to live the next time they come back and when they see an advertisement that is placed in a café, they might be more likely to keep that number handy for the next time they visit.

In this situation, you can then share your small URL or website link or even keep a bunch of visiting cards at the counter of the restaurant or cafe and ask them to hand it out to anybody who enquires about the flyer.

Special Offers

Special offers work like a charm and if you want to get repeat customers you may want to offer them a certain discount the next time they come and stay with you. You can also provide this discount to their friends and family members so that they help spread the word. You will be spending money on advertising and you will be paying bloggers or a cafe to put up your information in their space so there's no harm in offering a discount when you get repeat business. Airbnb has a referral program that helps hosts attract more customers to the platform so there is no reason why you shouldn't use your own referral program to get more people to come and reserve your property.

As a business, it is vital that you get into promotion and that's the reason why you need to focus on using the best possible techniques to promote and advertise your Airbnb listing. This will ensure that you not only get the exposure you are seeking but you also manage to keep your property occupied which will help you make more money.

CHAPTER 13

Airbnb Business Management

As an Airbnb host you are somebody who is not only earning a passive income, but you are also a business person. Once you look at your hosting service as a business, that's when you will realize the importance of the quality of services that you provide. As an Airbnb host, you are also required to provide the right management solutions to the business plan that you have come up with. If you have experience in running a business you don't need to stress too much because with a little effort and the right decision making, not only will you be able to run your Airbnb property like no other, but you will also make sure that you keep the guests as happy as possible. Here is a look at some interesting techniques for business management that come in handy for an Airbnb host.

Use Professional Cleaning Services

Airbnb hosts tend to try and save money by hiring cheap labor to get the cleaning done on a regular basis. This is something you should not compromise on because it is vital that you keep your property sparkling clean throughout the year if you want your guests to stay happy. Spending a little extra money on professional cleaning services makes a lot of sense after every guest checks out in case you don't have a professional cleaner who works for you.

Keep in mind that every little nook and cranny of the house should be cleaned perfectly and there should be nothing that is overlooked. As we have discussed before, there should always be two sets of cleaning done - one which is a basic clean and the other which is advanced clean, that needs to take place as soon as the guests leave the space. You should have a dedicated cleaning team working for you in case one of the crew is sick that way you always have a backup. As an Airbnb host you always look to grow and the best way to do this is to keep getting positive reviews from people in terms of the cleanliness and hygiene of your property.

Outsource As Much As Possible

Even if you only have one property that you rent out on Airbnb it could get difficult for you to constantly look after the guests when you have a 9 to 5 job. In this case, the best thing to do is to outsource most of the jobs to other people. You should always have a dedicated team who clean your property, someone who handles the supplies for the property on a regular basis, and someone who looks after the laundry. You will also need a caretaker; however this is something you can consider later on when you have multiple locations to handle or when bookings are constantly flowing in.

Use Accounting Software

It is very easy for an Airbnb host to believe that they can manage the accounts of the property without having to depend on any software to do the calculations for them. However minor expenses can lead to something really major and you'll end up with no profits unless you have a good accounting system in place. If you don't have one, you can always purchase one at a minimal fee so that you know that the rate you charged for the property, including the taxes, provides a certain profit margin even after all the other expenses have been taken into account. You need to make sure that you list every little detail in this account.

Set Aside A Budget Before You Start

An Airbnb listing may be free and you don't have to spend money in order to become an Airbnb host, however there are a number of expenses that come up when you decide to rent your property and this may be very unexpected so you need to have a certain amount of money that is set aside. Imagine the first time you rent your property the person destroys a few valuables. You could end up having a loss from the business just like that. If you want the show to go on, you must be able to deal with unexpected problems and overcome them as soon as possible. Before you decide to sign up as an Airbnb host, make sure that you set aside some money that you label as emergency expenses. While this money may not be needed, it's always good to have it handy and it's better to stay prepared. Even with profits that comes in, you should take out a certain amount of money and keep it aside for emergency funds. Later on the same money should be used for additional expenses like renovations or minor repair work that is needed around the property. When you do this you don't eat into your profit each time you do up the place.

Prepare Yourself

Being an Airbnb host is like starting your own business so it is important that you are prepared. If you have no prior education in business then get yourself a crash course on bookkeeping and accounting so that you know how to run a business efficiently. You might also consider reading a book on business management just so that you get the basic knowledge of what you need in order to get started without any problems. There are tons of books available at reasonable prices that you can get online and begin your learning process. Set aside a little time every day to prepare yourself to become a strong Airbnb host rather than rushing into the decision without any prior knowledge.

Get A Mentor

One of the best things to do when you become a host on Airbnb is to get a mentor who's been there and done that. If he or she is a super host, it will be perfect because they would have gone through every little process on Airbnb and would have seen the good, the bad and the ugly. A super host will not only enable you to understand more about Airbnb and show you how you can become a super host but they will also help you identify the shortcomings and how to deal with it.

Set Up A Separate Bank Account

When you plan on becoming an Airbnb host the most important thing you need to do is to set up a separate bank account for all Airbnb transactions. The reason this is so necessary is because if you use your same bank account that you use for every other expense, you will not manage to keep track of the money that comes in and goes out and you'll never be able to truly monitor your profits. The account that you set up for your Airbnb should only involve Airbnb transactions and nothing else. Even when you want to make certain modifications to the property you own, you should try to use your preexisting money in your Airbnb account and not touch any of your other earnings. When you have a separate account for your Airbnb money you will also be able to project certain expenses and you can see just how long it will take for you to purchase a new property. If you want to grow as an Airbnb host, your main aim should be to have multiple properties on the app.

Manage Your Property Online

Airbnb is a virtual application and the reason it is so convenient is because it helps you to save a lot of time. You can get a booking for your property without somebody actually physically visiting the property and this will mean that you can have someone book the property in as little as an hour. With this convenience in mind, you should try to manage everything that is related to your property online and this includes scheduling, cleaning, and even replying to messages regularly. If you have other applications or if you plan on going out of town during the duration that someone wants to come and stay at your property, this will not hamper any of your plans and it will also help you to seem more professional, thereby increasing the chances of you getting a higher rating.

Purchase Supplies From One Place

Look for a reasonably priced store and try to purchase all of your supplies from the same store. When it comes to purchasing these items, you may want to locate online solutions so that you don't have to stress too much about visiting the store to purchase these items over and over again. Make a list of the items that you purchase regularly and keep them marked as your favorite items so that you just need to reorder them the minute the supply starts to get low. Do not wait until the items are finished before you place your order. Make sure you place it when you know that you are running out of stock. When ordering items online take into consideration the shipping fee as well because these small amounts also need to be accounted for. A great tip that you can keep in mind in order to save money would be to use an Amazon Prime subscription so that you don't have to worry about paying any shipping.

Subscriptions

As an Airbnb host you may want to consider providing services like free Wi-Fi and subscriptions for apps which could include Netflix or Amazon Prime. Amazon prime is highly recommended since it helps to kill two birds at once. While you may consider these items as unnecessary expenses, they actually turn out to be better for you because people don't mind paying a little extra money for these services. When you are providing the services, you also need to make sure that all of them are paid up in full.

Get A Partner

If you know that you do not want to quit your 9 to 5 job anytime soon but you are enjoying being an Airbnb host, then you can always consider getting a partner. Many Airbnb hosts end up quitting because they don't have anyone to support them. If you don't want to spend money on a caretaker, then somebody who can assist you with the bookings and handle everything from start to end will definitely make a great partner. Airbnb allows you to add family or friends as additional hosts so you can add them to your listing and can manage everything for you.

Get An Investor

Like every business, Airbnb hosting also works really well with an investor. If you are doing great with one particular property you may want to consider a silent partner who helps you find a new property and increase your earnings. This can also work if you have the space available but no money for the new property.

This can work differently for different people. All you need to do is decide what you think will work best for you as an Airbnb host and apply those techniques to help you grow your business successfully.

Run Your Listing Like A Business

Airbnb makes it very easy to run your listing as a business. It has various marketing tools to make your listing stand out and a very easy to use calendar to make sure you plan your guests stay; it also keeps a record of all your transactions.

If you want to take things to another level then you will want multiple listings. We live in a 3 bedroom house but only use one bedroom. The rest of the rooms are sitting empty unless we rent them out which we do. We have listings on various websites and our price and reputation mean that we are frequently turning people down as we are full. We are also receiving guests who have stayed with rivals but prefer us due to comfort and competitive pricing.

You'll no doubt see that there are plenty of profiles in your area. When you are starting off, the real battle is to get noticed. Profiles of everyone, new and old hosts alike, are ranked on a number of categories which determine how high up the list you are. Some of these you can't immediately improve such as the number of reviews you have. However, all profiles are marked down if they do not respond promptly to inquiries. If you can, reply to questions and booking requests immediately but do it within 24 hours at the most. Longer than 24 hours will mean your profile will plummet down the rankings and to make things worse, your poor response rate will be shown on your profile which makes it less attractive to potential visitors.

Even if you have to turn down someone, try and take the time to draft a polite email as you can almost guarantee that a few months down the line, they will ask to stay with you again or refer a friend who is visiting your area.

Your listing can also sink down the listings if you cancel a booking or if there are disputes between you and third parties. Multiple infringements can mean your listings are suspended or permanently removed. However all is not lost if something goes wrong, as your profile rating is based on activity from the last 3 months and so if you hold tight and get back to doing things promptly you will soon see your ranking improve.

It's easy to get confused if you are running multiple room listings on multiple sites. I'd recommend doing a simple Excel spreadsheet that will complement the website calendars. Here you can keep track of when guests come and go, their contact details and how much money you make after deducting the nominal fees that Airbnb charges.

If you live in the United Kingdom, you are actually allowed to rent to your rooms tax-free each year to the value of over £4,000. In effect it's like receiving a large pay-rise that can buy you a holiday or two, go towards a new car or pay off a chunk of your mortgage. If nothing else, a regular stream of Airbnb guests will pay your bills so you can use your cash on more fun things.

It may be worth adjusting your prices at peak seasons like Christmas, weekends, or if there is a large sporting or cultural event taking place nearby.

Often when you have guests stay, they will come back again and again, especially if they are on business. It may be worth contacting the companies and organizations that they work for and letting their HR Departments know that you offer quality and comfortable accommodation.

This is especially useful for workers who are working in an office hundreds of miles from home or who are in the process of relocating. No-one wants to stay in an impersonal and lonely hotel week after week. Staying at your home will save them money and make you money and a long-term guest means you have less washing and cleaning to do. Many people can make more money by renting out one room to a business traveler during weekdays on Airbnb than others do by renting out an entire flat/apartment or house for an entire month. This leaves you with your home to yourself at weekends if you so wish or the ability to host some weekend sightseers.

This e-book doesn't claim to give anyone any legal or financial advice and it is important that you know your legal responsibilities, pay any taxes that are owed, and to keep good records, not only for official reasons but to make sure you are making the most money that you can. Depending on your personal circumstances, your council or landlord may not allow you to take in guests on short-term stays; this is particularly the case in some North American cities although the laws seem widely ignored and unenforceable. For your own peace of mind, you might want to check and adjust your insurance policies, especially if you have a mortgage.

CHAPTER 14

Building The Ultimate Host Profile

When you sign up as an Airbnb host your eyes will automatically get drawn to the super host program that Airbnb offers all its hosts. When you look at your competitors who are super hosts, you will go green with envy and you will want to become a superhost yourself. Is it difficult to become a superhost? Not really! Airbnb has very simple requirements that allows many people to become superhosts as long as they keep up to the expectations of the guest. All you need to do is have over 10 bookings in a year and get 5 stars for at least 80% of your reviews. You also need to have a high response rate of about 90%. The requirements to become a super host are not superficial and they are highly achievable as long as you follow through and consistently be a strong Airbnb host. There are various benefits of becoming a super host which is why it's definitely something you should consider doing.

To begin with, an Airbnb superhost gets a superhost badge that automatically gives people the assurance that the property is a good quality property and definitely worth renting. A super host also gets more visibility and a ton of benefits that help them to increase the number of bookings that they get on their properties. Once somebody sees a property listed by a super host, they tend to show more interest in it because it gives them the confidence that it is a good booking. Super hosts only need to remember that in order for them to stay as a superhost, they have to impress their guests and ensure that they keep up their hospitality skills on a regular basis. The advantage of being a superhost is that your profile automatically stands out among the rest of the profiles on the listings and your listing will get booked more often. Your property becomes a premium property and you can then increase the price because of the kind of services that you offer. You get travel coupons that you can use on Airbnb and you even have high priority support each time you call Airbnb.

The icing on the cake is that Airbnb hosts private exclusive events to which only superhosts are invited! If this doesn't get your motor running nothing will. When you sign up to be an Airbnb host for the first time, make sure that you set your target for becoming a superhost and increasing the number of properties you own. Not only will this help you to make more money it will also help you become a successful business owner and you will be happy and content doing what you do!

Superhost Evaluations

Airbnb evaluates all hosts once every three months. This is termed as the qualification period. This evaluation period starts from the first day of each quarter. The 12 months reviewed are calculated backwards from the date of review. This means that if the review period is 1st April to 30th June, then the 12 months being considered will be from April of the previous year to March of the current year. Once the host meets the qualification and performance standards, they become eligible to become a superhost. The status of superhost is automatically taken off if the host does not meet any of the requirements when the next review date comes. In such scenarios, Airbnb does not even inform the hosts that their superhost status has been removed. Some hosts choose to turn off their superhost badge even though they have earned it. Turning off the badge does not affect the superhost benefits that the host would receive. Irrespective of how well the host may have performed in the last 12 months, if they receive one bad review after becoming a superhost, their superhost status will be revoked immediately.

Conclusion

Starting something new may be an intimidating thought and a lot of people are quite skeptical about opening up their doors to complete strangers. However, considering the low rate of risk with Airbnb hosting and the number of benefits that it has to offer, there is no reason why you shouldn't consider becoming a host even though it means opening your doors to people you may not know. Airbnb not only helps you learn how to earn more money by using your property that was otherwise not helping you gain any financial benefits, but it also helps you to start saving towards the future and establishing something that you could convert into a business that can grow to be something big one day. Airbnb is a hassle-free service and this means you don't have to invest a lot of time to get the business up and running and the minute you learn the various tips and tricks that can help you to make the most out of your Airbnb listing (without having to take too much time out of your daily schedule), you will learn how to grow your business in the best manner possible.

There are a ton of people who have properties listed on Airbnb and earn over six figures from the multiple properties that they have managed to grow only because of being an Airbnb host. There is nothing that you need to do. It does not require too much effort, financial investment, or learning from your end. All you need to do is make the right decisions and this guide has it all covered with step-by-step procedures that will help you get started with your career as an Airbnb host and make you a successful host in no time.

It's not about jumping towards becoming a superhost today and forgetting about quality. It is all about learning how to provide the best possible service throughout your hosting experience so that people enjoy staying at your property and let other people know just how amazing their stay was. If you want to get something in return you need to give people something and that something should be a beautiful home and a comfortable stay. Being an Airbnb host doesn't require too much money. All it needs is the right planning and the perfection you will manage to achieve through trial and error. While you may end up spending a little more money than you originally expected to at the start of your hosting, it is something that you will eventually learn how to manage and you will find the perfect and most cost-effective solutions at the end of the day. Throughout this guide, you will come across various handy tips and tricks that you can use throughout your Airbnb hosting career. Not only will it help you to kick start your career but it will also help you grow from a single listing host to somebody who has multiple listings and is a superhost.

www.ingramcontent.com/pod-product-compliance
Lightning Source LLC
Chambersburg PA
CBHW021825170526
45157CB00007B/2690